ACCESS GRANTED

Tomorrow's Business Ethics

Patrick Henz

1.Edition (d), March 2017 – November 2019

Copyright © 2017, 2018 Patrick Henz, all pictures are copyright by Patrick Henz, if not other indicated. Published by aix books.

ISBN-13: 978-1544849829
ISBN-10: 1544849826

DEDICATION

To diplomats, hustlers, entrepreneurs and wanderers.

CONTENTS

	Acknowledgments	i
0	Introduction: The Future gets shaped by Artists and Scientists	3
1	Maslow or the Real Martian Pyramid	7
2	Pet Tech and the Dog Evolution	14
3	Compliance Internal Social Media	18
4	Startups: From Black Swans to White Unicorns	21
5	The Separation of Art from Craftsmanship	26
I	Interlude: Videogame	30
6	Chat-bots vs. Ethical Blindness	34
7	Compliance's Responsibility for Artificial Intelligence	39
8	How to Hack a Human	43
9	Gamification of Life	51
10	Job Profile: A.I. Compliance Officer	56
11	Borg	66
12	And They Dream of Electric Sheep?	69
13	Living in a Box	75
II	Interlude: Birth	79
14	The Forest	83
15	Modular Compliance	87
16	Trouble with Bubbles	92
17	Dark Matter – Dark Energy – Dark Net	95

18	A Playground for Compliance	98
19	The Rise of Electric Cars	101
20	Robo Advisors & Poker Players	106
21	Robots as Ambassadors for Humanity	110
22	Compliance 2025	113
23	The Cloud	127
24	How to Bribe a Robot	132
25	Swarm Intelligence, New Compliance Risks	140
Z	Conclusion: Computers are Useless	146
0	Bibliography	148
0	About the Author	152

ACKNOWLEDGMENTS

The book is a trip back to the future, as it combines visionary science fiction with actual technological developments. Besides all Artificial Intelligence, the focus is on the human and its relation to the technology, but also other humans. Robots, Internet of Things, Cloud, Micro-Learnings, Virtual Reality, 3D Printing and Self-Driving Technology are tomorrow's reality; risks and opportunity.

0000 0000 INTRODUCTION – THE FUTURE GETS SHAPED BY ARTISTS AND SCIENTISTS

Already back in 1956, author Philip K. Dick authored the short story *"The Minority Report"*. In a symbiosis between computers and human mutants, a special police department could get aware of crimes which would occur in the near future. This even, if the potential criminal not even started planning them or presented other criminal actions in the past. As science fiction journals had been popular in the 1950s, the story got published in *"Fantastic Universe"*. Philip K. Dick's work, often compared to Franz Kafka, became the base of several big Hollywood productions, such as *"Blade Runner"*, *"Total Recall"* or also *"The Minority Report"*.

In 2014, Stanford University conducted a comprehensive study about *"Artificial Intelligence and Life in the 2030"*[1]. As the results had been publically available, many organizations and companies used them as base for their own projects. One of these examples went effective in Dubai. Having access to big data, the local police department implemented a new software, what should connect, even potentially not related events, including the involved individuals. Based on this artificial intelligence, the sophisticated software should be able to forecast potential crime by these people.[2]

The *"Minority Report"*-movie predicted personalized commercials. Every time the main character John Anderton walked by such a display, a sensor recognized the individual and showed a commercial based on his profile. Even if this vision still not became reality in the city or commercial centers, inside the web it already became reality. Social media and web browsers collect the surf history, so that the different web sites present us exactly the commercials, from which media planners think that they are interesting for

---

[1] Stanford University (2016): "Artificial Intelligence and Life in 2030"

[2] MacDonald, Cheyenne / Best, Shivali (2016): "Dubai police launch AI that can spot crimes BEFORE they happen"

us. No need to say that these decisions are not taken any more by humans, but a software.

For product advertising this may be informative or annoying, but personalization of content goes further. Due to social-geographic facts or even potential political preferences, information portals and apps can present different news, photos and headlines. Even different versions of articles could be provided. This as user not only seek these sources to update their-selves, but furthermore to confirm their opinion. The danger of faked news is already publicly discussed, but in general the truth cannot be divided into black and white, but can be interpreted in many ways.

Such a technology would lead to a deeper split between the different sub-groups and foster parallel societies, which have less and less interchange of opinion and information. This effect gets fostered as individuals search for news not only to get more information, but strongly also to confirm his or her already existing opinion. As people already have elaborated opinions about most topics, they prefer the usage of information channels from which they estimate that the presented news is compatible to their already existing opinions. Information which are not compatible to existing opinions would be perceived as pushing the person outside its inner equilibrium. The individual is not comfortable in such a situation and seeks to get back into balance. To do this, an extended decision-making process must get executed. Such needs a look for all different type of information channels, so is only possible for important decisions.

An episode of the British TV-series *"Black Mirror"* presents a vision from the near future. Today's credit score, as known in the US, has been replaced by a friendliness-indicator, what reaches from one to five stars, remarkably similar as we know today from *"TripAdvisor"*, *"eBay"* or similar social platforms. This leads to that every person is chasing to get the maximum score, as this is required to buy a home in a nice neighborhood, able to get a rental car or even access to other people. If we think about it, we are not far away from this, as the business reality is changing, and more individuals start their one-person companies. Social platforms receive more power, as their ratings can build up or destroy individual existences. A high responsibility to protect against conflict of interest or cyber-attacks.

Not only is relevant how others see us, but furthermore our self-perception. Seeing the *"perfect life"* of friends and family on *"Facebook"* causes stress and envy for many users. Wrongly perceived as reality, and not the small part what others want us to see, the viewers feel the pressure of *"keeping up with the Joneses"*. Today this is a common idiom, but only few know that it comes originally from a 1913 comic strip. The newspaper *"The New York World"* published it inside their pages until 1940. Its main characters had been the McGinis family, who struggled to keep up with the lifestyle of this neighbors, the Joneses. Other explanations go further back in time, to the New York family Jones, wealthy thanks to their shares of the *"Chemical Bank"* and known for its extroversive lifestyle.

To keep up with social media connections, users present an artificial version of their real life. Starting with uploading only a selected version of owns life and going to an active alteration, what also includes the images. Today cameras, including smartphone ones, and apps can recognize imperfections and automatically fix them. This includes to bring the photographed person nearer to perceived *"social norms"*, as to change the color of skin or make eyes bigger. Such apps can be continuously used by the camera, it is only a question of time until individuals not only make belief their social contacts, but start to belief their-selves in these lies. Especially as the future may develop that people do not use big traditional mirrors, but instead an electronic one, consisting of camera and screen. Not unthinkable, as already today a large group of people do not use anymore the existing doorbells, but instead send a text message, when they are in front of their friends' house or apartment.

Patrick Henz

0000 0001 MASLOW OR THE REAL MARTIAN PYRAMID

The 1976 NASA Viking I-probe explored Mars by orbiting and later landing on the planet. Doing so, it took fascinating photos, which some of the viewers interpreted as faces and pyramids, especially in the "Cydonia"-region. Of course, these images inspired alien-theories and several science fiction movies, including "Total Recall" or "Mission to Mars". Later unmanned missions as NASA's Mars Global Surveyor (1997-2006) and the European Mars Express-probe (2003-) took photos from the same region, but the former artificial constructions had been identified now as naturally formed mountains, which based on the interaction between sun and shadow perceived like faces and pyramids.

1976: The Martian face, photographed by Viking I. Image by NASA/JPL.

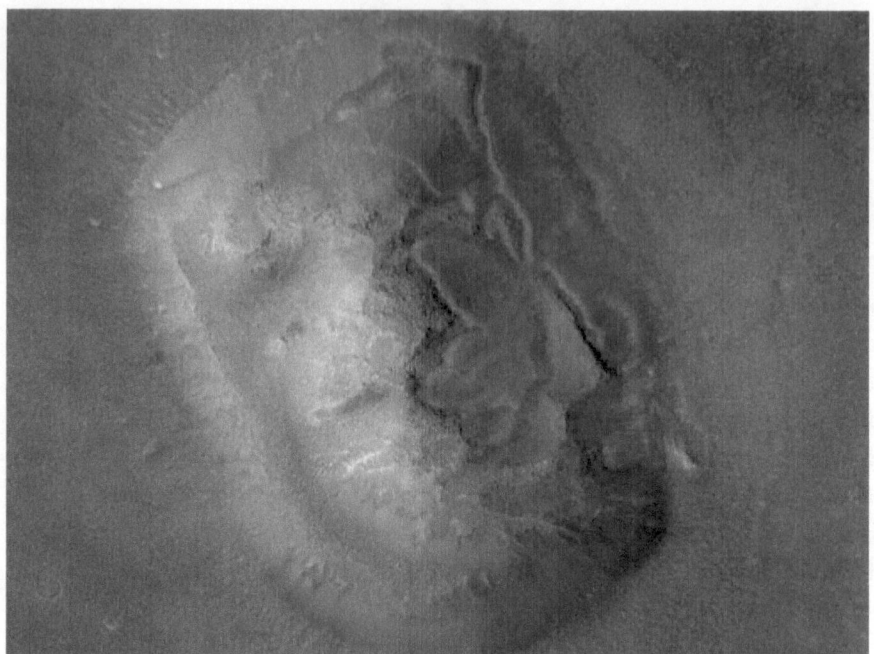
2003: The Martian face, photographed by Mars Global Surveyor. Image by NASA/JPL.

Today different governmental and private organizations are planning to return to the manned spaceflight. With exception of China, they are not planning to return to our Moon, but aiming directly to Mars. A challenging task, comparable to "Moon race" in the 60s, where John F. Kennedy gave his famous *"We choose go to the Moon"*-speech in 1962.

A manned flight to Mars still sounds like Science Fiction, but already Hollywood presented with "The Martian" a realistic outlook and most viewers understand that such a goal could be reached inside the next 30 years, meaning that the first human on Mars may already be born.

As such a unique mission requires a long-term preparation, different projects started not only to understand the logistical tasks, but also the challenges for health and psychology.

Who are the people already today are volunteering for such a mission? Ed Grann, fictive character of the 2016 National Geographic tv-series "Mars" brought it to the point: *"You don't go to Mars without ambition."*

To understand this better, we must go even more back in time; until the 1940s of the last century, but again it is the geometric figure of a triangle: *"The Hierarchy of Needs"* by the US psychologist Abraham Maslow. In this original model, also known as his pyramid, he is defining five distinct levels of needs. First the physiological, safety, social and ego needs; then the wish for self-actualization. Hereby we have the general idea that an individual first have to satisfy the needs from a lower level, before he or she feels the needs from the higher ones, for example first you must have something to eat today, before you want to ensure that you have enough to eat for the whole month.

For the crew of a potential mission to Mars, this classical interpretation of Maslow's Pyramid is not working. We can assume that such candidates are already on higher levels of the pyramid, at least on the fourth or fifth step, meaning the individual feels his or her physiological, safety and social needs satisfied. This as they are in the situation of a regular income, protected situation and social groups. For the individual, the mars mission supports to satisfy his or her individual needs, as finding a unique position inside the group and achieve other's respect. A group of people on the fourth level will, eventually lead to conflicts. Due to this, it is not only mandatory to simulate the mission to test the hard- and software, but also the crew.

The *"Biosphere 2"* project in the 1990s simulated a closed biosphere without any direct contact to the outside, similar to a potential Martian colony. The experiment should run two years, but the two attempts had to be stopped earlier. The first time due to low oxygen levels inside the biosphere and the second time based on mismanagement until potential sabotage of participating crew members. Even if the original time-limited could not be reached, both attempts gave scientists precious information, as the organizers of a flight to Mars are aware how difficult the mission is related its human factor and where things can start to go wrong.[3]

---

[3] Mellino, Cole (2016): "The World's Largest Earth Science Experiment: Biosphere 2"

A person being on the fourth step cannot be shifted artificially one step up or down, mission command must plan with a such a group and design the mission with as less points of conflict as possible. Furthermore, psychologist must work with the group and individuals to give them the skills to solve the distinct types of conflicts. If crew members are already on the fifth level of Maslow's pyramid, conflict potential is lower, as such individuals aim for self-actualization. They are not looking anymore for others' respect but want to bring their-selves to higher levels based on integrity, morality, values, creativity; and due to this collect valid experiences, which can bring the persons to these. Of course, there is no possibility that an external can promote an individual from the fourth to the fifth level, but it could be worked with the individuals to support them in reaching this level. The long-term preparation phase offers the possibility to give the participants positive and constructive feedback, so that they achieve the required external respect. Furthermore, conflicts can get simulated and different possibilities to solve them. Individuals must understand that the success of the group is the only way to receive also personal success.[4]

- **Self actualization**
- **Ego**   n
- **Social**   e
                       e
- **Safety**   d
- **Physiological**   s

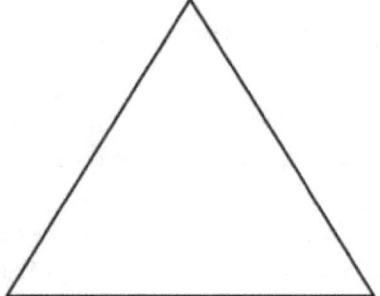

Maslow's Pyramid

---

[4] Henz, Patrick (2015): "The Geometry of Business Ethics"

Maslow introduced in a later model of his pyramid an even higher level, which he just described as "transcendence". A meta-goal, where the individual wants to become one with the earth, nature and universe. As this level is beyond logic, it may be a risk level for the overall mission, as an incompatibility between the personal values of the person and the perceived values of the mission may lead to an inner dissonance. This is a situation of discomfort for the person. An easy solution as walk-away from the mission is not possible, so that this may lead to conflicts, up to sabotage which may be risk of the highly fragile Mars-flight or –colony.[5]

To close the circle, in 2012 the NASA Mars Curiosity rover found on its way a 2,5-meter pyramid-like rock. Finally, we found such a structure on the red planet. For the usage and interpretation of Maslow's Pyramid it is important to understand that a human cannot be mapped in a simple model, but such a theory can show us tendencies. The average person wants to ensure the daily survival before he or she wants to plan the long-term safety of this situation. A person already being on the fourth level of Maslow's Pyramid or even higher may elaborate a preference of the higher levels in comparison of the lower ones. In other words, the members of potential flight to mars seek the satisfaction of their higher needs, even if they put their lower levels on risk. To be the first human on Mars, people would take on the risk of the flight and to never reach the red planet.

---

[5] Maslow, Abraham (1943): "A Theory of Human Motivation"

2012: The pyramid rock, photographed by Mars Curiosity. Image by NASA/JPL.

0000 0010 PET TECH AND DOG EVOLUTION

Between 100.000 and 15.000 B.C. the first curious wolf decided to get into a closer contact with humans. Most properly the still untamed animal saw the available food and the possibility to get such on a regular base from these strange creatures. With the time it overcame its restraint, visited more often the people and one day, continuously lived with them. As in a classic symbiosis, the relation offered more advantages than disadvantages, or in other words, a solution where everyone benefits. The wolf gave up its freedom to gain regular food, the humans had to share their limited food, but on the other hand, won an important guardian for their-selves and their livestock. The creature advanced from the first to the second level of Maslow's Pyramid.

So far, the starting point, but the relation grew further. The wolves not only gave up the freedom to run around wild with its fellows, it also laid its evolution in peoples' hand. As humans preferred intelligent, curious and calm wolves, they paired such; which led to the first dogs. They should not only be a guardian, but a real friend for its owners. This explains, why different dog breads not only became brave and strong, but others small and cute. Until today the pets are a relevant stress relief for their owners, which gets furthermore used by today's therapists. Studies confirmed that pets have a positive effect on lowering blood pressure, recovering from heart disease and even reducing the asthma and allergy risk in children, if they grow up with such an animal.[6]

---

[6] Junge, Christine / MacDonald, Ann (2011): "Therapy dog offers stress relief at work"

2016: Ewokie

Based on Statista[7], Millennials spent in 2014 an average of 7.43 hours online and the Generation X still 5,69 hours. Virtual social contacts replaced time that was spent with pets before. Stress relief is less possible, plus added stress factors appear as users fell the pressure of *"keeping up with the Jones"* or other successful lives of their virtual friends. Also, the Catharsis effect of videogames is still debatable.

Despite that owners spend less time with their animals, they continue to feel responsible for them. The human gets replaced by robots and electronic toys, called "Pet Tech"[8]. Similar to the iRobot vacuum cleaner, small intelligent machines throw balls for the dogs and for the short contact with the owner, the smart dog can use a WhatsApp tool and based on the human's decision receive a treat. The caring owner knows that the pet gets entertained, but the stress relief through the direct contact with the

---

[7] Statista (2015): "Average of daily internet usage worldwide in 2014, by age group and device (in hours)"

[8] Stern, Joanna / Barna-Stern (2016): "The Dumb, Delightful World of Pet Tech"

animal gets lost. Of course, this effect is also valid the other way around, dogs are a pack animal, so appreciate the personal contact with their owners, also to reduce their own stress levels.

0000 0011 Compliance Internal Social Media

As described earlier[9], Compliance communication is a sensible topic, as too less not serves the purpose to inform the employees and too much can easily lead to an information overload and that employees' ears get deaf for the message.

A solution is to create a communication strategy with tailor-made messages for the different internal groups. Doing so, everybody should receive the information what is needed for their job positions, not more and not less.

But communication (and this includes also training, workshops or the daily walk-the-talk) shall not limit itself to the transportation of information, but furthermore motivate the employees. This leads to the question what will we do, if we reached that goal and motivated employees ask for advanced information? We have to be honest and acknowledge that this could be always only a small circle of individuals, but nevertheless it is an important group, as they perceive the message not only as a legal requirement, but understand the ethical importance, not only for the company, but for the sustainable development of the region and their personal life.

The Ferrari Formula One-team solved the problem with an App: "*Scuderia Ferrari All Access*"[10]. Fans could download the software on their smartphone and register. When this was done, the users received access to a first level of information. When they liked and / or forwarded these messages, they gained points and with this liberated a next level of VIP information. For a higher level of access, users had to act as multipliers of the race team's communication. As they are emotionally involved in the sports, they did this anyway. The app supported the efficiency.

---

[9] Henz, Patrick (2016): "Compliance is a Race Car."

[10] Ferrari.com (2016): "Scuderia Ferrari All Access – The Team opens up to fans"

Today global organizations and companies offer a powerful intranet, which includes often also social media. Such a tool can be used as an internal LinkedIn or Facebook. If such a possibility is given, the Compliance department can and should actively use this.

Employees could join a Compliance group and receive here more detailed information. Such a communication channel cannot replace a classic communication strategy, as this information only goes to a group of self-selected employees. Due to this, the group will consist of individuals from risk- and non-risk-groups. Nevertheless, it is a relevant channel to be included into the overall communication strategy, as some groups, as the famous Millennials, are socialized with social media and may use this as their favorite source of information. If the intranet includes such a possibility, another possibility would be to write a regular Compliance blog. Important information could be included into the regular communication campaign and additional texts and photos could be included into the blog, which would be accessed by interested employees.

Like the Ferrari app, the highly involved employees actively seek information on these channels and act then as multiplier to communicate the gained knowledge inside their work and private groups.

0000 0100 Startups: From Black Swans to White Unicorns

In social psychology or science in general, a theory cannot get proved, only confirmed until someone else would disprove it later. Due to this, the statistical relations between corruption and the quality of education, quality of democracy or company behavior are confirmed, but not proven.

Black swans had been unknown in the Roman Empire and due to this, for its citizens it would had been a complete unexpected event to find such a bird. Therefore, the poet Juvenal used ironically this picture in the early 2nd Century A.D. to call a faithful wife a black swan.

Only in the late 17th Century, the Dutch explorer Willem de Vlamingh discovered such swans at the west-coast of Australia. The theory that black swans do not exist had been disproved, but nevertheless it stayed and since that day, it became furthermore a synonym for an unexpected event.

What about unicorns? They only exist in fairy tales or we just looked at the wrong places? These legendary animals had been reported from all over the world, in the antique India and Greece, in the Bible, and of course, since the Medieval Age furthermore in Europe. Literature described them mostly as a romantic symbol for the good, as in "The Last Unicorn" and in the dark science fiction movie "Blade Runner" it is a symbol for life and freedom.

The ancestor of our modern whale, the Cetancodonta, lived on the land, before a part of this group decided to return to the sea around 30 Million years ago. Interesting, the part who stayed on land became our today's hippos. These land animals are the closest living family member of whales and dolphins. The whale-family has many sub-members, one of them had been discovered in 1758 by the Danish zoologist Carl Linnaeus: the Narwhal.

This medium-sized white whale lives in the North (like different books, which define the unicorn as animal of the winter-land); in the Canadian Arctic, around Greenland and in Russian waters. Its horn, also known as tusk, is a type of tooth, what grows outside the mouth. It can get up to three meters, what confirms the existence of the Narwhal as the unicorn, even if it is a black swan.

US Venture capitalist Aileen Lee introduced in 2013 the "unicorn" as name for a successful startup company with a value of more than one billion US-Dollar.[11] If we see the high number of new companies, which never will achieve this size or fail in the their fist years, such a thing is really mysterious. In 2013 had been 39 unicorns worldwide, or in other words, 0,07% of all IT startups. Like medieval explorers, modern investors are hunting these magical creatures and speculate who might be the next Uber, Facebook or Tesla.

The Global Entrepreneurship and Development Institute creates the annual Global Entrepreneurship Index, what collects information on entrepreneurial attitudes, abilities and aspirations of the local populations and combines this with the social & economic infrastructure. The last includes the classic transportation, but furthermore also fast access to the internet. The 2017 edition of the index confirms the unicorn as an animal of the north. The six countries with the best environment for these mystical startups are the Unites States of America, Switzerland, Canada, Sweden, Denmark and Iceland.

If we compare the 2017 GEI Index[12] with the 2015 Transparency Corruption Perception Index[13] we achieve a correlation index of 0.91, what confirms a strong negative relation between entrepreneurship and corruption. This can be interpreted that in a transparent business environment the entrepreneur can concentrate on his or her vision of the business, and perceives less setbacks through corrupt officials and

---

[11] Lee, Aileen (2013): "Welcome to the Unicorn Club: Learning from Billion-Dollar Startups"

[12] Global Entrepreneurship and Development Institute: "Global Entrepreneurship Index 2017"

[13] Transparency International: Transparency International Corruption Perception Index 2015"

dysfunctional bureaucracy.

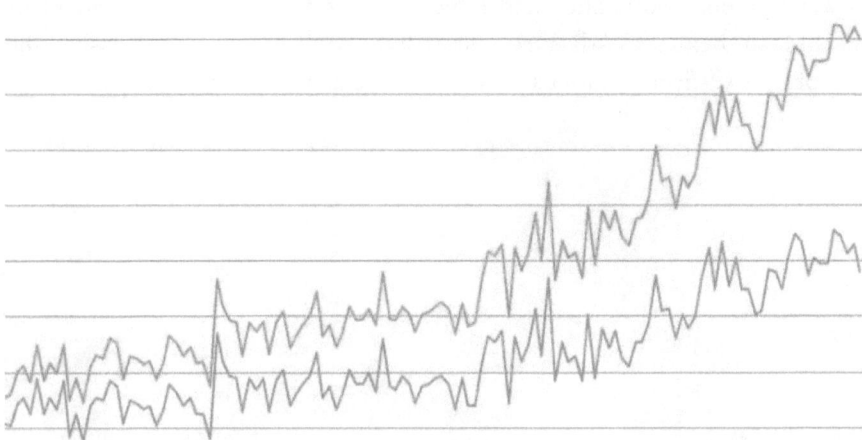

In Peter S. Beagle's book from 1968 *"The Last Unicorn"*[14], the magical creature needed a wizard for its protection. Like this, a startup is still not an established company and needs also such a figure. A Compliance Officer can support to set up a workplace environment with clear rules that apply for all employees. Furthermore, this defines and protects the individual's responsibilities and freedom; basic to ensure a creative environment. Steve Jobs understood this and once said: *"Apple is a disciplined company."*[15]

As most of today's startups are IT-related and include a young workforce, the Compliance Officer is less the traditional wizard, but more as *"Babylon 5's Technomages"*, a group of people, which use high technology to create magical effects and results. We are in a continuous technological revolution. Different experts predict that by 2025 30% of our today's jobs had been taken over by robots[16], what will include also Legal and Compliance positions. Due to this, such young companies will not build up anymore a big ethics department, but most probably limit this to one

---

[14] Beagle, Peter (1968): "The Last Unicorn"

[15] Henz, Patrick (2016): "Compliance is a Race Car."

[16] Elkins, Kathleen (2015): "Experts predict robots will take over 30% of our jobs by 2025 – and white-collar jobs aren't immune"

person, who can use advanced software to monitor third parties, manage training, elaborate a communication strategy and implement a whistleblower hotline. Compliance and ethics are not about laws and guidelines, but human beings. With being liberated from the standard tasks, the Compliance Officer can focus on the individuals and perform magic.

0000 0101 THE SEPERATION OF ART FROM CRAFTSMANSHIP

Pop artist Roy Liechtenstein is today most well-known for his comic art, where he converted imagines which perceived as directly taken from popular graphic novels, and painted them on a big canvas. His most famous paintings had been *"Drowning Girl"* and *"Whaam!"*, both from 1963. With this fresh style he became one of the founders of the pop art movement. The images may look simple in technic, but should not mislead the viewer. Lichtenstein enjoyed a traditional education in art. This with interruptions, as he served three years in the US-Army during World War II. He studied fine arts at the University of Ohio, where he received a Master in 1949. Cubism and Expressionism had influenced his early works. With the time he became fascinated by the raising comic and animation industry, so that he started to combine this with fine art. Thanks to his artistic background, he was able to simplify his paintings (similar like today Big Data gets resumed to Smart Data). Lichtenstein was not only creative artist, since 1960 he also lectured at the Rutgers University. In his following career he was not afraid to connect art and commerce, as he secretly hided comic characters in his art or in '77 designed a BMW 320i as part of the company's art program, which exists still today.[17]

Today's application *"Prisma"*, available for Android and iOS, took photo-software to a next level. Instead of using standard filter options, which each time use the same algorithms, the software is based on Artificial Intelligence. For its use, the app must be connected to the internet. The app it-self serves as a connection to the Cloud. To update a filter the program uploads the picture to the server. With scanning all images, the software learns from each use and due to this, each time applies the filter differently. So theoretically, if today you use the filter on a photo and you will repeat the same function next week, the result will differ.

One of Prisma's popular filter is "Tears", which in only a couple of seconds

---

[17] Berman, Avis (fetched 14.01.2017): "Roy Lichtenstein Foundation – Biography"

can turn every photo into a Liechtenstein-like pop art painting, no artistic skills are needed. This opens a question, who is the copyright-owner, the photographer, The Prisma company, jointly all Prisma users or even the Lichtenstein family (who manages the master's heritage)?

Independent from an ethics point of view, legally it is divided. The photographer keeps his or her rights, at least if this was given for the original image. Nevertheless, based on the use of the software, the software claims non-exclusive rights to use the created pictures with-out paying royalties:[18]

"Prisma does not claim ownership of any Content that you post on or through the Service. Instead, you hereby grant to Prisma a non-exclusive, fully paid and royalty-free, transferable, sub-licensable, worldwide license to use the Content that you stylize on or through the Service."[19]

Such provisions are like social media platforms, where the users provide similar rights to the platform. This opens the question, what about photos, which are meant completely for private use, where
   a) the user has no commercial agreement with the visual identifiable people ("model agreement") or
   b) uploads images from other copyright holders to just add for fun a filter.

What about the case that an individual uses Prisma to lay a "Lichtenstein filter" over the Mona Lisa? Prisma Labs, Inc. has the non-exclusive right for such an image? Complicated questions, so it is no surprise that you must be at least thirteen years old to use this graphic software.

These questions are relevant for all forms of art, as AI could support furthermore sculpturing (combined with 3D Printing), music or literature. Already *"Microsoft Office 2016"* included connection with the Cloud and intelligent services. For example, the software recognizes passive voice and

---

[18] Bader, Daniel (2016): "How to Use Prisma for Android"

[19] Prisma Labs, Inc. (2016): "Terms of Use"

suggests a sentence in the more attractive active voice.[20] In a potential next step, a software could analyze the writing styles of different authors and adapt a text accordingly. The prerequisite is given, Google already scanned more than 20 Million books.[21]

A German proverb states that *"Kunst kommt von Können"* (German for: *„art comes from can"*). Modern software changes the rule, as to repeat known art, classic education and craftsmanship lose importance. But this shall not mislead, as to invent new forms of art, such is still needed.

---

[20] Brandon, John (2016): "6 Amazing A.I. Tricks in Microsoft Office That Make You More Productive"

[21] Metz, Cade (2013): "8 Years Later, Google's Book Scanning Crusade ruled 'Fair Use'

INTERLUDE I: VIDEOGAME

Albert sat before the TV, but he did not see one of the science fiction series or any other program; since last Christmas he had one of the new video game consoles and was playing his favorite game. It was around a cute little round yellow character, who was walking around in his labyrinth, eating shiny little dots and while doing so, had to take care not to get caught by one of the ghosts.

Albert was in the eight level and using his last life. He directed the little yellow guy to the right, where had been the last dots. If he could reach them, he would, for the first time ever, reach the ninth level. But one of ghosts stopped this from happening and together with that the boy's dream of a new high score.

"Albert", it came from the dining room. Albert, how he disliked that name. Albert had been named old English butlers or even older German scientists, but it was not the name for a twelve-year-old American boy. His bad luck was, that his grand-father was called liked this and due to the family tradition, all first-born sons had been called as their grand-father.

"Ok, I am on my way", he answered as the game anyway just ended. After lunch he would try it again.

11pm, after Albert hunted for hours with his yellow friend through the different labyrinths, he was laying now in his bed. Even as he closed his eyes, he still saw labyrinths, ghosts, dots and power-pills. Tomorrow he would continue. Because of the summer holidays, he was sure about that! Most of his friends had been away and what else you could do in the suburbs than playing video games?

He was always hungry, a graving of video dots and power pills. Luckily you could find them all over the labyrinth. You only must reach and eat them. It would had been a real paradise, if there would not been these nasty ghosts. His stomach kept him going, these video dots had been too tempting.

Damned, there had been another of these creatures, but he could easily trick it. He left the labyrinth on one side and re-entered it from the opposite. These stupid ghosts fall for that old trick each time. Out of the sudden, he could see an enormous power bill in the middle of the labyrinth. Without hesitation he ate it and could hear a mysterious sound. At the same time all the ghosts turned into grey. He began to hunt them, also grey ghosts tasted good and furthermore, he was a real omnivore.

Two of his opponents he could snatch. He wanted to do the same with the third, as the ghost turned back into his original color. Unfortunately, he recognized this too late and the collusion with the ghost ended deadly for the poor yellow character.

Albert woke up. What a stupid dream! Perhaps his parents had been right, and he spent too much time before the TV. Anyway, without problems he was sleeping again and this time without any dreams.

11am, Albert had been there where he always was. Level eight, again shortly before reaching the next level. Only four more dots and no ghost could stop him this time. Still four, three, two, one, … He coped with the eight level, but instead as always to reach the next stage, it became dark before his eyes.

As he came back to his senses, he laid inside a labyrinth. He felt asleep before the screen and seemed to be again in the same dream. Not quite, this time he did not played the role of his favorite character, he stayed being Albert. He was not alone in his dream, as two ghosts came from the left. Due to this, he ran to the right and started to look back. The distance to the creatures became bigger.

The same as his idol, he wanted to trick them, leave the labyrinth at the right and come back at the left. The yellow one could do this, Albert not. It seemed that he hit an invisible wall. This hurt a lot. Strange, normally he should not feel anything inside a dream.

The ghosts came nearer, and Albert had the choice between up and down. He decided for the first option, as he saw his yellow friend there. He would help him.

As he was running to the top, he recognized that he became green as a power pill. What a strange dream. The yellow character smiled as he spotted the boy. *"Now I am saved"*, Albert thought. The yellow one approached and ate him, ultimately, he was a real omnivore.

0000 0110 CHAT-BOTS VS. ETHICAL BLINDNESS

Due to cost pressure, company's central functions must reduce headcounts. As technical development is progressing and Artificial Intelligence entering on all levels, such a re-structuring should be planned and executed before a potential economic downturn. This to ensure a systematic shift to Industry 4.0 and not just reduce personal and burden extra-work on the remaining employees.

To save money on the long run, such a change means an up-front investment, which requires that the company or organization is in a stable economic situation. As a considerable number of employees use smart phones, companies offer distinct types of apps for them. This includes travel expenses, HR topics, communication, but also Compliance. Today such tools are still quite simple, mostly the employee clicks through different menus to get an answer to a specific question or situation. If such pre-defined answer is not given, with one button the employee can call the responsible Compliance Officer. Such an app has two attractive benefits:
1) It ensures a 24 hours availability of Compliance knowledge, independent from the employee's location. As for the standard answers the app does not need an internet connection, it works even without a stable connection to the mobile network carrier.
2) Most employees received at least one Compliance training explaining the different guidelines and processes, for this there may occur a "too proud to ask"-effect, as the individual would have to admit that he or she forgot or not understood the provided information. This is a psychological pressure for all levels, but especially for Middle Management. A pressure which is less strong for low level employees and top management, as the first group does not have prestige to loose and the other one, thanks to the higher position, also on Maslow's Pyramid, is acting based on their own vision and values, so think less how other people may perceive them. An app offers a comfortable and anonymous possibility to get the required information without the potential perception of "losing the face".

Based on these standard functions, an app can go further and include a GPS-option. With such a possibility the software can automatically track the employee and provide precise information based on the country or region where the employee is at the moment. Today this GPS gets already used for travel-security apps, where employees receive automatic push-messages if a relevant event occurred near the user's location.

Artificial Intelligence is on the raise and chat-bots are already active in social media or the first line of customer service on company websites. These are text or voice related software, where the app can understand the user's statement or question and reply adequately to this. As part of the discussion, the chat-bot can learn from the user and include this new knowledge into the discussion, similar as a human would do.

Thanks to this modern software, users face increased difficulty to distinguish a human call center agent from such an AI program. Due to this, it is only consequent to use AI not only for the contact with customers or suppliers, but furthermore employees. This artificial colleague will take away workload from the human Compliance Officer. It can offer an individual treatment, with 24hours availability and given anonymity. The last at least, if the employee trusts in the company's data privacy processes. Such an intelligent app would not only serve as source for information, but furthermore can avoid "ethical blindness".

"Formally, ethical blindness can be defined as the temporary inability of a decision maker to see the ethical dimension of a decision at stake."[22] Often provoked by an employee, who is so much involved that he or she has no possibility to see the situation from another angle or point-of-view. One practical solution to avoid the problem is to ensure breaks, where the employee can discuss the situation with an employee of trust, friend or family member. If this is not possible, there should be time to sleep over a relevant decision or at least take a cup of tea or coffee. All these actions target to have a break in the flow, so that the individual can start a different (and more extended) decision making process, which may lead to different results. For the case

---

[22] Palazzo, Guido / Krings, Franciska / Hoffrage, Ulrich (2012): "Ethical Blindness"

that the employee is travelling in far-away countries, an intelligent chat-bot can take the role of a human discussion partner; understand the risk situation and argue from a value point-of-view. Furthermore, it serves to disrupt the continues flow of the employee and provoke the required break so that the employee can (self-) reflect about the situation.

Such an AI should clearly not replace a human Compliance Officer as building up a trustful relation needs "face time". So even if modern IT supports, the Ethics & Compliance department needs an adequate travel budget to meet employees on their work location, this includes office, workshop or project. An AI not even should pretend to be human. Voice communication and recognition may help for the interchange of information and build up a trustful relationship with the AI, but actual studies and even Hollywood movies confirmed that for this it is not required that the human perceives the AI or robot as human.[23] This is true for the outer appearance or the software's avatar, but also affects the direct communication. As example, today we enter efficient search-strings into the web-browser to find the required information. Like this, we may use a similar language to talk with an AI, instead of using sophisticated sentences as we do with other humans.

If not prevented by data privacy law and / or internal guidelines, such app could connect to the HR-database and gain access to the employee file. With this access the software understands if the individual is intro- or extrovert, success seeker or failure avoider. Thanks to more information the software can adapt its behavior and actively manage a distinguished discussion. This functionality needs an open discussion about ethics and if everything what could be should also be implemented or not.

The AI does not only analyze the users' written or oral communication to understand what kind of information he or she is searching for, but could go a step further, to conclude from the construction of the sentences or changes in the voice to the individuals emotional state. Facebook uses this technology to detect potential suicidal tendencies at their users.[24] If we have

---

[23] Henz, Patrick (2016): "Compliance is a Race Car."

[24] Knight, Will (2017): "Andrew NG Has a Chatbot That Can Help with Depression"

a situation that values and behavior are not compatible, the individual feels being outside its normal state of harmony. Based on Leon Festinger's "theory of cognitive dissonance"[25], now the person perceives an inner pressure to get back into harmony again.[26] Such cognitive dissonance leads to negative emotion and could be detected by the chat-bot. If the software combines external databases (for example the Transparency International Corruption Perception Index), with the employee's location and state of emotion, it could conclude that the employee perceives him- or her-self being inside a stressful situation and start related actions, such as direct communication or even alert headquarters. Elevated level of stress limits or even blocks the employee's possibility to execute an adequate decision-making process. If the chat-bot has access to the individual's body values, as for example heartbeat, it can take this information also into consideration to come to more precise predictions.

---

[25] Festinger, Leon (1957): „A Theory of Cognitive Dissonance"

[26] Fischer, Lorenz / Wiswede, Guenter (1997): „Grundlagen der Sozialpsychologie"

0000 0111 COMPLIANCE'S RESPONSIBILITY FOR ARTIFICIAL INTELLIGENCE

In 2016, the American Citibank conducted a study together with the prestigious Oxford university. Based on its results, 47% of today's job inside the US are on risk to get automated, in other economies as China, the risk of automation is up to 77%.[27] With such numbers it is clear that this wave is not limited to the typical blue collar-worker, but furthermore targets white collar-positions. Modern software cannot replace top decision makers, but their direct assistants. Due to the study, only 3.5% of lawyers are in risk of getting replaced by AI, but up to 94% of paralegals and legal assistants.[28]

Due to this, Compliance must prove itself as independent function, which in opposite to Legal is, first, not about laws and documents, but the employee. The focus should be on active prevention of corruption and other wrongdoing. So far Compliance's responsibility is to the human employees. But what about Artificial Intelligence?

The European Members of Parliament is discussing to analyze the legal status of Artificial Intelligence and robots. It should be defined what rights and responsibilities have *"electronic persons"*.[29] If such a such status gets established, a company not only has responsibility for its human, but also artificial employees. As complying is the result of according behavior, Compliance should take responsibility.

---

[27] Grut-Williams, Oscar (2016): "Robots will steal your job: How AI could increase unemployment and inequality"

[28] Price, Rob (2016): "Stephen Hawking: This will be the impact of automation and I on jobs"

[29] Griffin, Matthew (2017): "Robots to get legal recognition as Europe vots to classify tem as 'Electronic persons'

An early psychological approach is the *"black box-concept"*, what admits that we do not understand how an individual takes its decisions, but only measures what stimuli had been perceived and what behavior this triggered. This approach is valid for human and artificial intelligences.

For the human employee, trainings and documentation explain the company's guideline, which the individuals must follow. The black box-model does not further distinguish, if the employees follow because of the fear of punishment or because they believe in these laws and guidelines. The regular controls should ensure compliance and that violations lead to disciplinary sanctions.

For artificial employees a similar approach can be used, only that such software or robots do not attend personal or web-based trainings, but receive the guidelines as part of their programming. This requirement will create new job-profiles, as Internal Auditors or also Compliance need employees, which can understand the used software and databases.

If the software is self-learning, the task gets challenging. Besides to focus directly on the AI, Compliance's target group are the programmers. It is relevant that they are involved in the company, including living the company's culture. As it is true for human employees, the responsibility of a software must be limited. In practical business life, the software may take decisions alone, but severe decisions have to the confirmed by a human. Decision making can be defined in mathematical formulas. The decision with the highest expected outcome will be chosen. Business always means to take on risks. In 99% of all cases a decision leads to a positive result, but in 1% not. Knowing such mathematical relations, the programmers can create the software as *"success seeker"* (taking on higher levels of risk) or *"failure avoider"* (being more risk-averse). Unconsciously, such a decision may depend not only on the company's vision, but the also the programmer's character.

In 1984 an Artificial Intelligence conquered the TV-screens. The anarchic Max Headroom first stared in the British television-series with the same name, and later also became the host of music-show. Due to the limited technical possibilities at that time, it was no real software, but still a human actor with a strong makeup. Based on the basic programming and the gained experience an AI software becomes an individual, as no software will be identical to another. For this, a one-time admission as for a standardized product as a car is not enough, each AI software needs individual attention to ensure that based on the learnt, it still shows the required behavior and decisions. Just such its human colleagues. This is especially relevant, if the machine learning is not limited to save the learnt and use it for the required behavior, but go one step further that the software can change its own code or the code of a different software. As utopic as it sounds, the University of Cambridge together with Microsoft experiment in this direction. With *"DeepCoder"* they already presented a first demonstration. A potential use of this technology can be that it will get easier for people to get into programming, as the software would automatically do the complicated coding.[30]

The Compliance tasks may change with such technological challenges, but as it is a part of the evolution, Compliance can adapt to this or if not, gets distinguished and replaced by other corporate departments.

---

[30] Futurism (2017): "Our Computers Are Learning How To Code Themselves"

0000 1000 HOW TO HACK A HUMAN

1 Social Engineering

The human brain is still the most effective super-computer. Yes, artificial computers had been able to beat their human competitor in single tasks, as for example winning a game of Chess, but if the same computer receives a different task, as playing cards, the computer does not know how continue, as it does not have the relating software. Chess is indeed a complex game; different strategies offer a higher number of possibilities. Nevertheless, the rules limit the game, it is not comparable to a chaotic environment as real life.

Despite its capabilities and flexibility, like its artificial versions, also the human brain can be hacked. Social engineers take advantage of this, for example with phishing mails and calls.

Cyber criminals prepare for their attack. In social media, as Facebook, LinkedIn or Twitter, many individuals transparent their-selves. This is precious information what the criminal mind can use for a faked contact. Further important for the attack are psychological biases to put their victims under pressure. With this the criminals want to push them outside their personal comfort-zones. In such new situations the individual has no ready-made protocols how to react, and suffers of a higher level of stress. This stress may block or hinder logical thinking, as the individual tries to return as soon as possible into its personal comfort zone.

Social engineering can be understood as hacking the human brain. Public information, as found on social media, are used to create a realistic story, what the criminal must implement into the head of his or her victim and then active it there. The more personalized the story, the more realistic it sounds. This is like a computer hacker who is trying to reach the same result with a software virus, like a Trojan. Based on different psychological biases, the human hacker understands different pressures may lead to misbehavior. To reach such, there exist different strategies:

- *"I can resist everything except temptation"* is a famous quote by the Irish poet and author Oscar Wilde. The classic phishing emails present a situation that a person in a developing country wants to get a higher sum of money outside its borders and needs the help of the victim, as a bank account has to be opened and the victim to invest first, before he or she, would receive a relevant part of the treasure. Again, the email creates a certain level of urgency, but furthermore it pretends that the recipient is in a situation of extraordinary luck, as like a lottery-win fast money is possible. The message describes a win-win-relation, what creates a situation of trust. Doing so, mostly it is clear to the reader of such an email that doing as requested would be an illegal act. This is relevant, as even if the recipients fall for the message and sends several thousand dollars to an unknown back-account, he or she will not report this later to the police, as it would had been a part of a criminal scenario as money-laundry. Furthermore, people felt ashamed that they had been fooled so easily.

- In more sophisticated fraud attempts, the author of the phishing email or caller pretends to be a higher lever manager or client. In the *"Stanley Milgram Experiment"*[31], participants executed the orders from a perceived scientist, even if these had been against own knowledge and values. In the setup of the experiment, the participants had been instructed to give a raising strength of electrical shocks to a potential other participant. This other person sat in a different room and the participants had only audio contact. The participant had not known that this other person is part of the experiment team and, had been an actor and not received any shocks at all. With the raising strength of potential electric shocks, the actor simulated raising pain and requested the participant to stop. The potential leader of the experiment (the *"scientist"*) ordered to give more and stronger shocks and many participants continued until the person from the other room stayed silent. These results had been shocking, as it showed how easy it may be to get individuals to obey, even if this would mean to hurt or kill others.

---

[31] Milgram, Stanley (1963): "Behavioral Study of Obedience"

There had been later also critics to Milgram himself, as he let the participants to cross certain lines and showed them their inner abyss.

Based on the knowledge of this experiment, the criminal mind takes advantage of this psychological pressure and request the victim's support, even if this would mean bypassing of internal guidelines or external laws, like making a transfer to another bank account as originally agreed on. The interaction with a person who stands on potential higher level in the business relation means stress. To foster this effect, such a phishing email could take advantage of other known stress situations. For example, the hacker would send it out at the annual end-of-year of the company or the tax-return season.

- The criminal can also use an opposite tactic and present him or herself as in a weak situation to create pity. Important is to create, as far as possible, a realistic picture in the head of victim. Such a strategy gets used for a phone-call than a faked email, as this strategy is needing a discussion between the criminal and the victim. Building up such a picture can be reached with the tone of the voice, underlined with sound-files as a crying baby. Such sounds can be easily found in the internet, as for example in YouTube. The created stories are taken from real-life, so that the victim feels empathy, especially as he or she already had been in such a situation or can imagine to be one day. Therefore, the person is willing to bypass internal security processes and may give out even confidential information. Important is that the caller has the capability to keep up the vivid picture in the head of the recipient. This imagination works like an app or a computer virus inside the brain and let us execute behaviors, which are against our own interests. Already a brief time after we answered to such a call, the power of this *"virus"* weakens and the individual receives his or her first doubts and starts to regret the actions.

For the typical cyber-attacks, the subscribed anti-virus services offer in a relative brief period an adequate protection against the new attacker. Similar must be done also for the human brain, even if this is more challenging than just to implement an update of the existing software.

- A first relevant step is to make employees aware of the different psychological pressures and biases. Everybody can be a target and in risk to get manipulated. For training purposes are different informing and entertaining videos on YouTube.

- The company must define clear guidelines and limitations. Such regulations do not limit creativity and invitations, the opposite, it defines a clear space, where the employee knows that he or she is safe to act. When red lines are communicated, there is no grey area, where the employee felt alone and is not clear what the company expects.

- Employees of all levels should be empowered and feel free to ask management or request management decisions. The tone should be that everybody is responsible for his or her decisions, not only management.

- A training should present stress relief-tactics, as include breaks into the workflow, even if this would mean only five minutes. All kind of interruptions serve to reduce the risk that employees may get rushed into a wrong decision.

2 Cyborgs

Cyborgs are defined as humans with robotic parts. This is in opposite to an android, what is a humanoid-looking robot. Even if the concept came from science fiction and is mostly still here to find, cyborgs are already living among us. Most of them updated their-selves to overcome a natural desadvantage, as for example color blindness or even blindness in general. But other individuals use the technological possibilities to enhance them with senses, completely new for humans. Such new senses are part of an artistic movement, as the example of the Spanish artist Moon Ribas, who implemented a chip to add a seismic sense.[32] Thanks to this technology she is connected to a mobile app and can feel in real-time earthquakes, independent where they are on planet. Based on cyborg philosophy, a human can , supported with implemented high-tech technology, reach a closer relationship with nature and planet Earth.

As it is true for all processes, the more we switch from manual to IT-managed process, the more vulnerable is the organization. As, forecasted by William Gibson in his book *"Neuromancer"*, the cyborg-trend should continue. It is only a question of time, until Governments identify this as possibility to influence and / or manipulate individuals.

In the time of the Cold War, from 1953 to '70 the CIA experimented with *"MKUltra"*, what should support interrogations and torture. These mind-control techniques should be used against soldiers and spies from the Soviet bloc. The project was based on the idea that natural and artificial drugs, including LCD, should control the individual, so that he or she behaves against personal interests, values and interests, in favor of the organization or department, what administered the drug.

Implemented chips can give relevant information or directly stimulate emotions, consciously or not, they can have the same effect as today's drugs. A hacker can use the wireless connection between the implant and the cloud to hack the individual. A color-blind person could be shown other, darker colors, what may lead to depression. Faked information of super earthquakes can lead to panic, especially if the cyborg has no possibility to deactivate his or her implant.

3 We are the Cyborgs

Back in 1839 the US author and poet Edgar Allan Poe authored his short story *"The Man That Was Used Up"*. Better known for his tales of horror, he took this time the focus on another topic, as he wrote about a fictive meeting with the war hero *"John A.B.C. Smith"*. First, he had been

---

[32] Quito, Anne (2016): "Sixth Sense – This woman, a self-described cyborg, can sense every earthquake in real time."

impressed by his outer appearance, then later he saw that these looks had been based on technological spare-parts. Smith literally had been used up by the different battles, so that legs, hair, eye and even his palate had been artificial.[33]

The term *"cyborg"* had been formulated a first time in 1960 by the scientists Manfred Clynes and Nathan Kline. It describes a human individual with artificial parts. This to replace missing ones or to achieve enhanced abilities.

If we take a fresh approach, we understand that already much more cyborgs exist todays than we thought of. In a study from 2016 researchers from the universities of California, Santa Cruz and Illinois found out that increased people depend on the internet as resource of information. Today's schools and kindergarten bring children early in contact with computers and the internet. Instead of pure fact learning, today's students learn where to find information and how to access these databases.[34] With this, today's students have access to more information than any other generation before them. Due to the pure number of information pure fact learning cannot work anymore, and other factors as accessing the information and an adequate processing process become more relevant. The internet became an external extension of our brain. Even if individuals do not have any physical updates on their body, information storage became outsourced, as we perceive to be in a continuous connection to *"our knowledge"* on the net.

Due to the lead investor of the study, Dr. Benjamin Storm, memory is changing. If we need to answer a question, we use less time to remember the required learnt information, but more access the internet to let Google or Wikipedia find *"our"* information.[35]

---

[33] Poe, Edgar Allan (1839): "The Man That Was Used Up"

[34] Taylor & Francis (2016): "Cognitive Offloading: How Internet is Increasingly Taking Over Human Memory"

[35] Taylor & Francis (2016): "Cognitive Offloading: How Internet is Increasingly Taking Over Human Memory"

This requirement of the modern age is on the other hand a risk factor. The individual perceives the internet, especially his or her preferred pages, as source for objective information, but they may be flawed based on the author's opinion. Even worse, employees may be let to pages, including Twitter and Social Media, which communicate fake news and information. Less than information inside a book, articles on the internet, included encyclopedias as Wikipedia, can be changed from one moment to another, including that such changes is not easily detectable for the reader.

For most of the topics, individuals only feel a low involvement. This makes perfect sense, as the regular visit at the supermarket cannot lead for each buy-or-not-buy to an extended decision-making process. This opens a risk that information for low level-decisions get not questioned and used. If slowly step by step such information gets altered, the individual would not recognize the changes and this may lead later to decisions, which are not compatible anymore with the person's original values. As consequence, the individual changes his / her decisions or even values & attitudes.

The individual uses information from the open internet, but also from a protected Cloud. In opposite to its name, the information does not flow through the air, but is stored on one or several physical servers. With this, it is target of the known cyber-attack and data privacy risks. Mostly discussed are the risks that non-authorized (or even authorized) users steal the stored information. But hackers may work less obvious. Like a Trojan virus, what stays non-active for a period inside the system, a hacker can unrecognized alternate information and databases, so that the person uses this incorrect information for their decision-making process. Such a virtual attack can have relevant consequences in the real world, as in critical decisions the individual, based on altered information, takes the wrong alternative. To avoid the risk to not fall on flawed, manipulated or biased information, individuals must keep an adequate level of skepticism. We may outsource information, but not morality.

0000 1001 GAMIFICATION OF LIFE

Generation X is the first one, who could had been grown up with video games and home computers; even if not from early age on. The following Generation Y includes digital natives, as the usage of computers had been widespread since the time of their birth. This includes that in their teenager years social networks had been en vogue and the rise of YouTube began. The actual latest Generation Z is growing up in even a more virtual environment.

- Fast and reliable internet is 24 hours, and thanks to smart phones and tablets, independent from the location available.
- Amazon, Apple, Netflix and YouTube make video content always available. The importance of classic TV-stations is going down.

Due to this omnipresence of content, questions and answers, the individual perceives less requirement to investigate topics and even the need to "wait for answers".

The study "Culture Wires the Brain: A Cognitive Neuroscience Perspective"[36] confirmed that the human brain adapts to the environment. Big parts of Generation Z used a smartphone since early age on, as stressed parents discovered that YouTube videos may calm down a toddler. Designers created apps for this young target group to stimulate early development. A first step to get them into video games. Thanks to this early introduction to the virtual world, the brain adapted to the requirement to concentrate on a screen and its changing and animated content. As downside of this development, it gets more difficult for the human being to stay concentrated on just one topic. Most young employees work multitasking, concentrating on a longer topic or a single topic may bore them. The frontiers between work- and private-live are luring.

---

[36] Park, Denise C. / Huang, Chih-Mao (2010): "Culture Wires the Brain: A Cognitive Neuroscience Perspective"

Due to this, employees are expecting more from their job than just money; it should have a purpose based on the individual's values, and important, it must be challenging and so, entertaining. From the socialization with video games, young employees are used to switch from level to level, each time getting faster and more complicated. A classic final opponent must be overcome to reach the next step on one's career-level. The virtual world needs less physical status-symbols as a big house and car; what makes young employees more independent from a job and for themselves easier to quit a position. Instead of this, experiences are an import motivational factor, as participation in challenging projects, travels and a positive work-atmosphere. Even virtual "likes" can be perceived as a motivational factor. Work-life-balance does not only mean to spend more time in home-office, but also that the office gets more "home-like".

Furthermore, affected is corporate training. Web-based training, but also in-person workshops must include gamification. The presenter shall not give answers, but the participants must elaborate them their-selves through discussions and analyzing different cases. It can be compared to the first Jurassic Park movie, where the Tyrannosaurus Rex declined to eat the tied sheep, but required to hunt down its food.[37] It may sound contradictory to compare Millennials or Generation Z with dinosaurs, but in opposite to the general opinion, dinosaurs had been a very successful species, who ruled the world for around 170 million years. Online training can follow the technical possibilities of actual video games. Why not let the employee create an avatar and present the learning topic in a 3D-environment?

Modern work has changed, and administration jobs adapted and often got reduced. Many tasks have been automatized and employees work multitasking. Work reality plus the attitudes of young employees often avoid that online-courses get done in one attempt. More often an employee starts and stops, when a new task comes in. Concepts as *"micro learning"* may fit for today's and tomorrow' workforce. Short 5-10 minutes learning episodes, which the employee can take between different tasks, or even as break between a bigger project. With this, they can support to get the

---

[37] Crichton, Michael (1990): "Jurassic Park"

employee out of the routine and to avoid ethical blindness. Such micro learnings not only can be used to transport information, but also to foster values, attitudes and desired behavior. It targets cognitive structures, but also triggers emotions.

Corporate trainings and especial micro trainings may get combined with another trend, Artificial Intelligence. Such a software can identify the actual tasks, experience, knowledge and even attitude of each company' employee and create tailor-made communication and trainings. This may be a modular-based online-training, or also one-on-one communication via email or the organization's social media intranet.

On the other hand, trainings (on- and off-line), which work with gamification, also include risk factors. It must be found an equilibrium between game and information:

- Game > Information: If based on the offered entertainment the user does not receive the information, the basic requirement of the trainings was not achieved.

- Information < Game: If the game is not entertaining and / or includes an information over-load, the user does not get motivated to play. In this case, no play means no transfer of information.

As rule of thumb, the content of information inside a gamified training is lower than a *"normal"* presentation. On the other hand, based on the higher attention level, the provided information is more likely to get perceived and learnt.

Gamification does not only support to provide information, but also to raise the motivation-level. In a technical, social or business simulation the user gets in charge. Based on his or her decisions, the airplane arrives correctly on the terminal or the country's economy is prospering. If an employee understands not only laws and guidelines, but their purpose, including what would be the consequences of violating them; his or her general involvement level raises. Higher involvement leads to higher identification with the company and its values.

As trainings always have a motivational factor, they try to lead the employees to a wished behavior. This includes a grey factor where motivation ends, and manipulation starts. Presentations have the power to present information and potential relations as logical, even if they are not true or at least not proven yet. This is possible in a traditional PowerPoint workshop, but even easier to create with gamified computer trainings and may get multiplied if Virtual Reality is involved. Related to cyber-attacks and social engineering, the company has an interest to create smart individuals, which are less likely to fall for such attempts. But furthermore, each employee should prepare him- or her-self for that, as such manipulation attempts may occur also in private life and even by the own employer.

0000 1010 JOB PROFILE: A.I. COMPLIANCE OFFICER

The Smiths asked in 1985 *"How soon is now?"*. Regarding robots and Artificial Intelligent the answer is *"very soon"*, already arriving. Another relevant question about the internet is *"Where is now?"*. The Internet world penetration rates are uneven. Based on numbers from December 2016, 88.1% of people living in North America are connected, on the other hand only 26.9% of the population in Africa.[38] Around half of world is not extensively using the internet so far. Furthermore, the regions their-selves will be diverse, not only in developing countries, but also in the potential developed world. Talent is available all over the planet, so it is to be expected that small *"Silicon Valleys"* will appear on all continents. This will be a motor for the local markets, but also lead to a further internal separation of societies. Nevertheless, the future already started.

Today's pupils and students may work later in jobs, which do not exist today. This based on the trend that technology is replacing humans on certain positions, independent if it is in the workshop, factory or office. Based on the international accounting network BDO and its survey[39], today around 40% of in-house counsels already use an electronic review assistant. Such a software reads and understands contracts to highlight important parts and propose changes, based on local law and company policies. Today the software is an add-on, but it can be expected than in several years intelligent software has the capability to replace human employees in the Legal department. Like today's known customer service, the software will be the first level of review and control. Only if the software identifies special risk factors, it would send the document to the second level, which would be the human contract manager.

---

[38] Internet World Stats (fetched 14.03.2017): "Internet Usage Statistics"

[39] Livni, Ephrat (2017): You next lawyer could be a machine"

On the other hand, this development will need new jobs, one of them could be an AI Compliance Officer (AICO). This as intelligent software enters the offices and with the time replaces today's human colleagues. But AI will not only be our internal partner, it will be included in our products. This opens the requirement that a Compliance department not only guides and controls the human employees, but extends its services to the artificial ones.

To support with these tasks, the university- and business-workgroup *"Fairness, Accountability, and Transparency in Machine Learning"* (FATML) identified five areas to ensure responsible decisions making by Artificial Intelligence software: Responsibility, Explainability, Accuracy, Auditability and Fairness.[40] These areas give a first insight into the tasks of the AI Compliance Officer.

1 Responsibility

A robot or intelligent software is less comparable to the humanized *"C3PO"* or *"R2D2"*, but better be understood as the *"T-1000"* from the *"Terminator"*-cinemalogy. Originally created to kill all humans, but as the resistance could kidnap one of these machines, they changed the basic programming to implement the new goal to protect humans. Doing so, the machines could learn and adapt to different situations, but nevertheless stayed true to their basic programming. This is like a circus tiger, the animal can learn tricks from the tamer, but nevertheless stays a predator. If such an animal would hurt or kill the tamer, it is not to blame, as it is part of its nature. Accordingly, if a T-1000 hurts or kills a human, the machine is not to blame, as it is following its basic programming.

This makes it clear that the Ethics & Compliance trainings are not assisted by the robots and computers, but the human programmers. The AICO should be part of the Compliance department and not IT. Sensibility is needed as the target group programmers and software designer are an internal department without regular contact to suppliers or clients.

---

[40] FAT/ML (2017): "Principles for Accountable Algorithms and a Social Impact Statement for Algorithms"

Nevertheless, they must be emphatic to understand the social and legal impact of their software.

An easy example is the dilemma of self-driving cars, as in the particular situation of an accident the software must decide if it should drive the car either into a group of people or as alternative against a single person. Due to US-law it may be adequate to steer the car against the single person to limit fatalities, in opposite to German law, where such an active decision may be judged as murder. Legal, but also Ethics & Compliance, must be involved in the development of AI products, so that they can counsel the programmers about such relevant algorithms. If the software is finished, it requires a robust protection as, for example, the buyers of such self-driving cars are tempted to include legal or non-legal updates to ensure that the car protects first of all the people inside the car, and overrides a potential algorithm that always searches for the alternative with the least number of fatalities.

ACCESS GRANTED - Tomorrow's Business Ethics

2004: Urania-Weltzeituhr, Berlin, Germany

As we know from our today's computers and smart phones, updates are quite frequent. This is not different for AIs, just the opposite, here are two different cases:

- The human programmers change the basic algorithms to include enhanced functionality or eliminate an existing bug. If the behavior of the AI could have a social or legal impact, such updates would need a Compliance approval. To ensure this, the company must implement an effective approval process, including to archive the received electronic signatures to transparent the change history.

- AI means that the software not depends on its programmers to learn, but can do this on its own or via the Cloud in connection with similar software and / or machines, at least as today we automatically connect Artificial Intelligence automatically with Machine Learning or even Deep Learning. If a relevant number of AIs take part, such machine learning can happen fast. The basic programming must ensure that even with the added information the machine will obey its original purpose and values, as defined, for example, by *"Asimov's Law of Robotics"*. If the machine operates in a sensible field, it may be discussed, if the software includes a filter so that the newly learnt does not get automatically included into the potential behaviors. This may be especially needed, if the software learns from others via the Cloud, as different countries and regions need to obey with different laws. Furthermore, the ownership of information must be defined. If for example, machine A is connected with machine B, but both belong do competitors, Antitrust laws may prohibit that the machines learn from each other, as it could get interpreted as interchange of relevant information.

Responsibility includes being prepared for different emergencies. Employees who get aware of corporate wrong-doing need access to an anonymous whistleblower-hotline. Furthermore, like potential tornado, earthquake or other natural catastrophes, the company shall have different processes for the potential wrongdoing of an AI, including accidents caused by such.

2 Explainability

The coding process starts with the idea what the AI should be capable of. Based on this vision, the programmers create the software based on mathematical formulas. In an ideal world the AI works as predicted. But, of course, this never happens. A program is complex and often distinct parts contradict each other and lead to malfunction. A certain part of the programmers' tasks is an old-fashioned "try-and-error". With the changing of variables, the software finally might do what it should do. Despite the positive output, the solution is not explainable. In the normal day-by-day no problem, but if the software faces a demanding situation, its behavior is not predictable and may violate ruling law. Due to this, it is imperative that the software is explainable, documented by the responsible programmers and audited by the AI Compliance Officer.

It would be beneficial, if the AICO masters coding and could *"read"* a software. Furthermore, case studies may test the software to analyze, how it reacts in special situations, which are out of the ordinary.

3 Accuracy

The programmer's attitudes must be compatible with the company's values. They believe in the organization's vision and want to work inside the guidelines. Of course, this not automatically means that the later software will elaborate inside these permissions. Coding errors may lead to violations of internal guidelines and external laws. Similar as human employees (including their behavior), who are included into the company's control system, the same must be valid for their artificial colleagues. Real-time monitoring, or at least sample checks, must be in place to ensure compliance with relevant laws and regulations.

A risk factor is *"temporary fixes"*. Especially as in the software industry it is common that the users practically get used to finish testing the program. This can be openly communicated as a public beta version or less visible as a *"buggy"* version 1.0. It is common that thanks to the available internet, updates come quite regularly, automatically downloaded and installed. People are in average more tolerant about errors in a non-tangible software than in tangible products, as a house or refrigerator. Especially a risk for companies which started as pure software houses, but then extended their portfolio to offer also physical products. Or the other way around, traditional companies work together with software companies to implement software and artificial intelligence into their products. Two different corporate cultures may collide.

An AI Compliance Officer should check the software, including how it would react in different case studies. A part of such a control should be further to detect *"temporary fixes"* and the agenda when these should get replaced with a final solution.

The error-margin must be analyzed to understand the consequences. For example, a 99% annual-internet availability sounds good, but means to accept four days a year without connection.

A real-time monitoring of the AI should inform the relevant levels of the organization's management. Not only to present the problem, but also that they are able to react, what could mean shut down the software and conduct the process manually. It is imperative that an emergency plan has the protocols how processes would work *"manually"*, without AI.

4 Auditability

AI, as all software, is based on mathematics. On paper, this makes it auditability. The AI Audit- or Compliance-department should include employees, who are able to read the software's code to understand why the machine is acting as it does. With this, artificial employees are more transparent than their human colleagues.

Understanding human values and attitudes is most of the times like a black box. We know parts of the input, as for example communication and trainings. The company's different internal controls, for example related to gifts & hospitality, can check the output. Bills and invoices serve as documented behavior. What is invisible are the processes inside the employee that lead to this behavior. Social- and business-psychology supports us to assume what may happen inside the individual, but it is not readable as a software-code.

Even if software is more transparent than the human mind, it should not be underestimated that experienced programmers may find possibilities to hide and encrypt code. This makes it difficult to audit or analyze it. Again, this underlines why it is imperative that the programmers work based on the company's values and follow the guidelines.

5 Fairness

As today's society is diverse, AI should be able to attend all human counterparts in fair way. Fairness can be defined that everybody should have the same opportunities. On the first view, a clear mathematical formula should not violate this, but Albert Einstein already said: *"Everybody is a genius. But if you judge a fish by its ability to climb a tree, it will live its whole life believing that it is stupid."* To reach such kind of fairness, empathy is needed. To ensure that an intelligent software has this quality, the responsible group of programmers should live on and include such values. A company must carefully select its employees, this also means the individuals for the IT department. As it is true for all teams, the IT groups should not only include the most talented individuals, but also ensure that the different characters are able to interact as a team. Diverse backgrounds and personalities may support to shape a team out of a group. The importance of fairness in AI is understandable when we see the actual Microsoft Office package.

"Word" can more than the known functions to detect errors in the different languages. It goes further, the software can automatically change passive voice into the more positive perceived active voice. It is thinkable that the software would exchange single words to foster known stereotypes or even censor the author. Similar is true for different camera apps, which can automatically adapt skin colors. To ensure that AI complies with diversity, the company must monitor the software, but also to focus on the programmers. These people must live based on the company's values.

Even if the algorithm for decision making is elaborated, the quality of the results depend on the input of information. The AI Compliance Officer must ensure that the flow of information is adequate for the software. Furthermore, even if the AI itself is strongly protected against hackers, the flow of information is a risk-factor, as part of them public (as taken from news portals or social media), so a potential target for hackers or even censorship. The AICO must review or even audit the quality of information and the IT department will be key contact to discuss potential weaknesses. All involved employees must take ownership of the required and used information.

0000 1011 BORG

If something goes terrible wrong in a company and a FCPA investigation started, the potential offender often explains that he or she thought to have acted on the company's best interest. *"Bribery had been the only way to assert in a hostile environment and compete against unfair clients & competitors."* Coming from such a philosophy, it is a crude awakening to see that not only the government treats the individual as a criminal, also the own company itself does not protect him or her. Just the opposite the organization, to protect itself, will try to present the case as one renegade employee acting against company values and rules.

Conducting business always means taking on risks. This is unavoidable, only question is, what will be the risk-level. This is a management decision and gets confirmed by regular risk assessments. The results are incorporated into guidelines and processes. These documents define where the red line is. Doing so, the guidelines define furthermore the space, where the employees can safely act and perform their tasks. Inside these limits, the employee can be sure that he or she acts in the company's interest. For this, it is imperative that the organization adequately communicates this, including live these decisions via a *"walk the talk"*. It must be clear that guidelines are not a recommendation, but an internal law, an imperative! If such a message is not given, the single employee must interpret the situation him- or herself. Especially in difficult environment this may lead to misinterpretation, as for example, *"paying a bribe would be in the company's interest."*

Independent if a clear tone from the top exists or not, an organization has as priority to protect itself. If needed, this includes that a single member gets sacrificed. A graphic example is the Borg in the Star Trek-universe. This alien race is conquering big parts of the galaxy and each civilization on the way gets assimilated. With this, people lose their individuality and instead become a small part of the collective awareness. But even this mighty power may lose single units or battles. To ensure the survival of the collective, single members had been sacrificed and left behind.

To settle a FCPA case, the investigated (and potentially guilty) company must cooperate with the US Department of Justice, what not only includes to allow access to all company information, but furthermore to inform the investigators which employees violated the laws, including names and other relevant information. With this knowledge the US department can open a civil lawsuit against the indicated employees. Company lawyers have their duties to the company and are not allowed to counsel the investigated individuals.

"Every employee is responsible for his or her actions." This is not only a phrase, but an important truth, what should be internalized and work as an *"ethical vaccination"* against ethical blindness. If employees act against laws and values, a *"I do it in the company's best interest"* is no more a valid excuse.

0000 1100 AND THEY DREAM OF ELECTRIC SHEEP?

Androids, human-like robots are in development, but still for the next time science fiction. Nevertheless not only futurists and philosophers think how a society with humans and robots would look like, but already the European Parliament elaborated a resolution to define robots as *"electronic persons"*.[41] This document acknowledged that intelligent software and robots are in the process to get more independent and there is the possibility that they will elaborate self-awareness. Circumstances, which today are only known from humans and a limited number of animals. This raised several ethical questions how to treat such machines or even non-physical software, but long before this will be acute, there are more practical questions, as taxes.

As AIs are property of the user or cooperation, they do not receive a salary. But on the other hand, they already started to replace human employees. Different countries discuss a *"robot tax"*, what companies should pay to compensate for the missing income-tax. So far, the contra-side has still the majority with the argument that such a tax would slow down the technological development. But the pro-side gets momentum with prominent supporters as Microsoft founder Bill Gates, who especially argues that the technological development needs a soft brake to ensure that the society has the possibility to adapt to this relevant change, as its need to create the required jobs for the unused human resources. A proposed robot tax or other changed tax constructions could support that the region does not lose its source of income and furthermore, that the next generations receive the required education to work and live with these robots.

---

[41] European Union (2016): "Draft Report with recommendations to the Commission on Civil Law Rules on Robotics"

Nevertheless, as former Greek Finance Minister Yanis Varoufakis pointed out, such a robot tax is a too simple approach for a complex development. In the near future, a robot or AI software still does not include self-awareness and, due to this, no ego. They will not go on strike or treat to leave for another company. So, there are no regular loan negotiations. In the moment they replace a human employee, there can be calculated a theoretical loan sum, but there would be no realistic loan development for the machines. We must be honest; they do not receive any salary. Furthermore, not all AI / robots will replace humans, so here we do not have a mathematical base to calculate such a potential salary. Automation started at the end of the 19th Century, since then machines always replaced humans. So why it should be different today that companies should pay taxes for an intelligent software? Already fewer smart tools as the first "Office"-package replaced human assistants.[42] More revolutionary approaches as a Universal Basic Income (UBI) are tested in societies as Finland & Canada. Here it presented positive results.[43] Nevertheless these regions are transparent and advanced, so other countries may experience fewer positive results. The idea is that the total output of country gets taxed, independent if it is produced by humans or machines and, based on formulas, get distributed to its citizens. This does not mean that everybody gets the same, but can depend on indicators as the persons experience, weekly working time or education level. Along this, it may include social factors as personal requirements. Of course, a country may experiment with hybrid models, as having an UBI plus individual salaries. Such a model would be like the ideal as we know it from the Star Trek-movies and – series. Everybody works in the area where he or she is interested in, salary is no topic. But we must be realistic, UBI needs efficient and transparent governmental structures. Finland and Canada traditionally are top countries in the different anti-corruption indices. The required distribution proposes a high temptation for corruption and bribery, so in higher risk countries it is to estimate that relevant sums would end up in obscure channels. A risk that was relevant to bring down most of the socialist systems at the end of the 20th Century.

---

[42] Varoufakis, Yanis (2017): "Taxing robots won't work, says Yanis Vaoufakis"

[43] Galeon, Dom / Marquart, Sarah (2016): "Finland isn't alone in trialing a universal basic income, Canada is trying it as well"

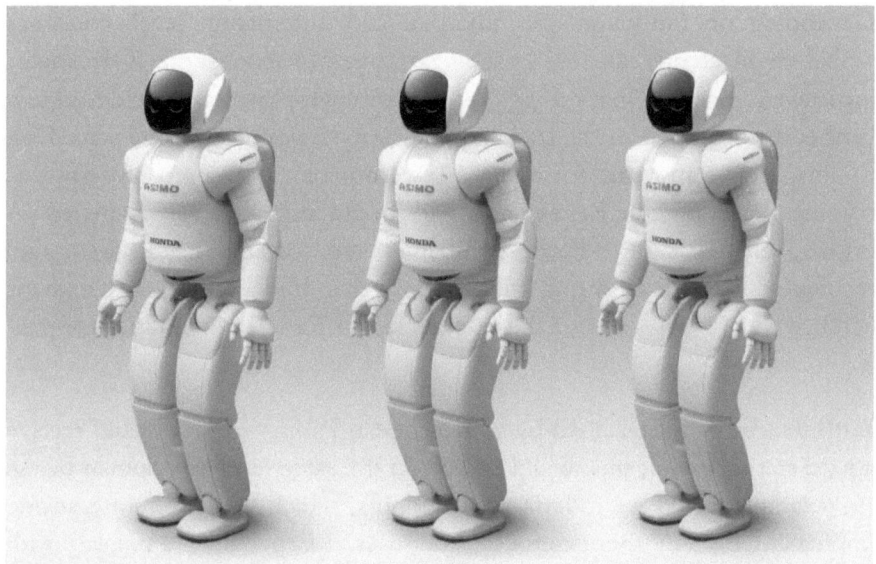
Honda Asimo, press photo

We have to say goodbye to our romantic idea that the intelligence of a robot would be inside his or her human-like head. More likely it will be like smart phone apps, which already exist today. On the phone is only installed a small program, which lets the user access a network and connect to the Cloud. For example, a weather app. The installed software can recognize where on the planet is the user and he or she can request the weather for a defined time and place. The weather forecast will be elaborated on the central or decentral computer and then displayed on the mobile phone. Accordingly, computers and robots will not be intelligent their-selves, but achieve this thanks to the connectivity to the Cloud.

The German electronic music pioneers *"Kraftwerk"* had since decades the idea to retire as human musicians and instead let real robots perform on the stage. This with the vision to abandon the organization of a classic tour and travelling from one location to another, but instead perform concerts at the same time in various locations. AI, connected via the Cloud brings us one step closer to this vision, especially as the robots could be all connected and so could learn from the feedback from crowd A, even if they are performing for crowd B and C.

Depending on the actual job structure and automation level, countries would be differently affected by the next wave of robotization. A decline of income tax together with raising numbers of unemployment would lead to a further drifting apart of the societies and support populistic politicians. Due to this, it is important for today's government to be prepared for this coming development. Resistance to it should not be underestimated. A positive change culture inside companies and societies needs focus and resources. A new society must find an answer to the question, how humans can live with dignity, even if the society does offer less possibilities for paid work.

With the resolution planned by the European Parliament, AI would receive a legal status, even if this would not be on the same level as a human being. An example could be today's animal rights, which are differently strong implemented in the various countries. Especially animals with consciousness should benefit from a defined autonomy and dignity. With this, animal rights are in opposite to the common legal interpretation that animals are treated like goods.

Today such robot rights are a preparation for the future, as consciousness in an AI was still not confirmed. All human-like behavior is part of primary programming and imitation to ease the interaction between man and machine. This imitation supports a humanizing of the machines, but in opposite to animals, intelligent software does not perceive pain or fear. Today a machine can get deactivated without ethical doubts. There is still no discussion that machines should not be owned by humans or an organization.

Another practical topic are insurances. As AIs get more independent in their work, monitoring must advance. On the other hand, even if machine learning can adapt based on different experiences, a software cannot get held responsible for its actions. It is inside the company's responsibility to conduct a risk assessment and understand what internal and external stakeholders can be affected by potential malfunction of the software. Based on the result, the AI / robot can be insured.

An interesting point is that specialized software may outperform human specialists, as computers already beat their human opponents in Chess and other games. But it is not limited to games, some white collar-tasks can already be performed by AI, faster and with a lower number of errors. Even if intelligent software cannot be legally held responsible for its decisions, due to its overall quality in the decision making, a company would give such software a certain independence, even for decisions regarding external stakeholders, as for example implemented into the service to customers. This is a calculated risk factor. Even as the AI decision making process itself maybe superior to a human one, nevertheless it strongly depends on the information input. If information is filtered based on a political or whatever other bias, the regarding decision can be sub-optimal. The same risk as it exists for a human decider. For the best results, Artificial Intelligence needs to be in a free and democratic society, with access to a maximum of information. Based on this understanding, AI software is vulnerable to hacker attacks. Even if the software itself maybe be difficult to hacked, a potential intruder may alternate or limit the information stream. If information is manipulated and the AI would only decide on half of the truth, the decision may be completely wrong. As the British poet Lord Alfred Tennyson once said: *"A lie that is half-truth is the darkest of all lies."*

As AIs do not possess self-awareness, they are an emotional-less witness. Smart voice-controlled devices find their way into modern homes. There they are connected to the net and registered cloud services. It is to be expected that soon we may control our smart home thanks to these small devices. Thanks to their name and friendly voice, we are tempted to humanize them, but it must be understood that they are machines. As part of their tasks they record the human interaction with the machine. This information is stored in the Cloud and in case of a legal search warrant would be handed over to the police. This process is not new, also telephone- and internet-providers hand out information in case of an official investigation. The AI has no personality to deny such a handover of information, there is no emotional relationship with its owner. Due to different local laws and the situation that the information is stored outside the country, this may lead to contradictory demands and friction, as the local law may require the handover of stored information, but the data-privacy law of the country where the physical server stands, forbids such an action, at least if the suspect would not allow it.[44]

At last, a robot declaration can work as a *"quality seal"* and ensure that the intelligent software and robots of the region act based on the values of the society, what may include compliance with *"Asimov's Law"*. If the government does not take time to define the future, there is the risk that other countries will do so, especially as software is not restricted on physical frontiers, but acts inside the net and Cloud.[45]

---

[44] McLaughlin, Eliot (2017): "Suspect OKs Amazon to hand over Echo recordings in murder case"

[45] European Parliament Research Service Blog (2017): „Have Your Say On Robotics And Artificial Intelligence!"

0000 1101 LIVING IN A BOX

The next step from Artificial Intelligences with self-consciousness is the theoretical possibility that we are living inside a computer-generated simulation, as we know from the *"Matrix"*-trilogy This can include that we are living in a gigantic *"Truman Show"*, setup by a higher intelligence or even go further that we are nothing more than software our-self and so our whole existence is only virtually.

The last idea already had been simulated with the 1985 game *"Little Computer People Project"*, where a human character lived together with his dog in a house inside the computer. The user had the opportunity to interact with this virtual lifeform via the telephone or a typing machine. The concept advanced to the 2000 title *"The Sims"*. Similar idea, but 3D graphics and more possibilities for interaction.

Supporter of the "simulation"-theory present as confirmation the so-called *"Sims Effect"*. The widely known situation that you sometimes enter a room, but cannot remember for what purpose. A potential explanation could be that we are living inside such a virtual game and a user controlled us to this room without our own will.

As fantastic as this hypothesis sounds, there are acknowledged scientists, who take it into consideration, as the astronomer and moderator Neil deGrasse Tyson. This can include that we would be part of a simulation by other civilizations or even our own, thousands of years in the future. As we discuss that robots and AI could develop self-awareness. The creators of the simulation could have reached this task and we are the result.[46]

Startup pioneer Elon Tusk goes a step further and stated that the most probable explanation for the circumstances that we not would live in a simulation would be that humanity is the first civilization in the universe

---

[46] Moskowitz, Clara (2016): „Are We Living in a Computer Simulation?"

and no others have invented simulations yet.[47] As surreal as this is, the hypothesis is hardly to disprove and may impossible to confirm. Scientists argue that a simulated computer cannot have the same processing power than its original. Such differences would be very minor and only detectable with the highest technology.[48] At least, if our creators not programmed us to oversee such an evidence.

What would be the purpose of such a simulation? There are different options:

- Science: Archaeologists do not limit their-selves to digging out artefacts or study ancient books. To understand how people lived in the past, it is important how they created these artefacts. Often such processes are not completely documented. The only way to understand this, is to repeat the process and experience it in person. For this, professors, students and other interested parties use historic tools and try with them to rebuild traditional houses, wooden ships or other objects. This method not only allows to understand how the tools may had been used in the past, how long it took to build the object, but furthermore collect similar experiences, including feelings, as people hundreds of years before.

    Thanks to sophisticated computer technology, future generations may conduct such studies inside the computer, with a highly detailed simulation. This possibility is known as the "ancestor simulation".[49]

- Decision Making: "Virtual Twins" are en vogue, as such models depict real machinery or systems inside the computer. Based on truthful information, companies get better insights into the equipment's efficiency. Before the original process gets changed, potential consequences get simulated inside the computer. As

---

[47] Hern, Alex (2016): "Elon Musk: ‚Chances are we'll living in a simulation' "

[48] Cain, Frasier (2017): "We are Living in a Simulation?"

[49] Bostrom, Nick (2003): „Are you living in a computer simulation?"

humans, and all other living things, are part of the system, it is understandable why it must simulate them as well.

In the 1989 game "SimCity" the player could build up from scratch his or her own city. When houses and infrastructure had been erected, the Sims came and inhabited the place. They acted autonomously, and if the infrastructure did not fulfill their needs, catastrophic traffic and demonstrations had been the result. To speed up the process, the user had the possibility to set the time on double or higher speed. Thinking about tomorrow's processing power, we could live in such a fast forward-mode, meaning that 1000 years for us, just would be one hour.

- Gaming: Besides science and economics, simulations get used for gaming. Our only purpose is the entertainment of a far-advanced civilization. If we see the success of simulation games, another possibility.

Today's discussions around Artificial Intelligence include the possibility that such a software or robot may achieve self-awareness. An intelligent creature does not inevitability need a physical body, but could be a character inside a simulation or live in-between the computer and physical world, thanks to Augmented Reality or even the hologram technology.

"Blade Runner 2049"[50] is not only the successor of the first Blade Runner-movie, but also loosely based on Philip K. Dick's book "Do Androids Dream of Electric Sheep?"[51] In the movie from 2017 appears a character named "Joy" and the audience is puzzled, if she developed self-awareness or is just a program following its given algorithm.

Ironically, Dick said 1977 at a conference in France: *"We are living in a computer programmed reality"*. He never used this conviction for one of his books, but it can be concluded that the Wachowskis saw this interview and used it as inspiration for "The Matrix".

---

[50] Villeneuve, Denis (2017): "Blade Runner 2049"

[51] Dick, Philip K. (1968): "Do Androids Dream of Electric Sheep?"

Patrick Henz

INTERLUDE II: BIRTH

Birth

It was an uplifting moment. Despite my still young life, I could perceive directly after my birth already everything clearly. Now I laid in a bed, directly beside my mother. *"Hello, my little one"*, she said to me. *"Enjoy your life here, you only will have 30 years."* Strange words for a newborn. I still thought about it for a longer time, but could not make sense out of it. It is okay, I still had my whole life before me.

7 Years

It was a strange celebration. My family and I went all the way from Venus to Earth for it. My mother told me that it was my uncle's death party. But this was illogical, he was still young, it only would be this 30th birthday. Further oppressive the atmosphere, everybody dressed in black, only his uncle all in white. During the evening I had the opportunity to speak with him. To find a calm moment, we went to garden of his house, the two moons shined bright over the night sky. *"Uncle, you have to die?"*, I asked him *"Yes and no"*, he answered. *"On the one hand I have to go in two and half hours, but on the other one, I will begin to live."*

I did not understand, he still looked full of life. The strange thing about death was that you could calculate the moment, up to the second. 23:07:42 should my uncle leave out of this world. Shortly before that we formed in the garden a circle around him. We took us on the hands and started to sing. Exactly at the calculated time he just vanished. It was the end of the party and somewhere in background I could hear the silent roar of a dragon.

14 Years

Based on the pure power of my thoughts I travelled to the Jupiter moon Europa. The idea was to pass my summer holidays here. One morning I sat at a lagoon to watch a unique spectacle. 27 silver UFOs raised and sank into the ocean, dancing on the above the waves. It was a wonderful week then I enjoyed life.

21 Years

Nothing is more beautiful than the birth of a new star. For one year now I was travelling through the galaxy based on the power of my thoughts. I saw if before, but always such an event was amazing for me. Together with a dozen other lifeforms, watched it from a safe distance, around one million kilometers away from the young star. I wished that my parents could see me, I enjoyed life.

28 Years

I knew that my time was slowly coming to an end. My health was still strong, but anyway, there had been no sicknesses. They never existed and never will. Only a few mavericks told me about. Nevertheless, I only believed what I could see with my own eyes. Still I had two years, as with exactly 30 years all men and women vanished from this world. To be alone for the day, I spent it in the middle of a black hole. Einstein was not right, also here time passed by, as I could hear the ticking of my watch.

Death

My death-party had been on island named Atlantis. With all the ruins it was ideal for the ceremony. Everybody came, my wife and children, also all the rest of my family. I had to think to my uncle's last words, was there another life? Soon I would know it. 14:43:59 and I started to dissolve. Total black war around me, there was nothing more. Around one hour I stayed in this situation before I started to hear voices. Out of the sudden I saw a blending light. It was strange, artificial. There was a lamp hanging on the ceiling. I was in a kind of bed. A man in white doctor's coat said, *"You can go now."* Outside the room waited a woman, around 50 years old, my mother. *"Come"*, she said to me, *"we have to go to a birthday party."*

It turned out to be mine. Like all humans, I spent my first 30 years inside the cyberspace, today was my birth. In a free minute of my party I went into the garden. Something strange happened, something penetrated my nose. I bent down and saw an unimpressive flower. The first time after thirty years I was able to smell, and it was even more beautiful than the birth of a start. A man stands behind me. As I turned back, I saw that it was my uncle.

0000 1110 THE FOREST

Based on history, Germans have a special relationship with their forest. It was here where in the year 9 the Germans let by Arminius won against the legendary Roman legions and still today 32% of the country is covered with forest.[52] So it is no surprise that a German poet defined the proverb *"can't see the forest for the trees"*. Christoph Martin Wieland (1733 – 1813) brought a known phenomenon to the point, due to the many single details, an individual is often not capable to perceive the overall-concept. This is less an intellectual limitation, bur furthermore a combination of different psychological pressures, as for example group-, performance-, competition-, time-, role-, location-, authority- or conformity-effects. Different psychologists confirmed these biases in their experiments. The interaction of these single effects can lead to the situation that *"good people do bad things"*, better known as *"Ethical Blindness"*.

A subject not only for scientists, but also artists took this topic. Robert Smith from the Cure worded it in 1980 as: *"Into the trees, suddenly I stop, but I know it's too late. I'm lost in a forest. All alone"*. A perfect description for Ethical Blindness. Due to the problem to not perceive the forest because of the surrounding trees, it is easy to do a step into a wrong direction. With each step forward the individual is slowly leaving the path of laws and guidelines. Going back to path gets each step more difficult, as the employee must admit the violation and disciplinary sanctions may be the result.[53]

---

[52] Bundesministerium für Ernährung für Landwirtschaft (fetched 24.2.2017): Waldland Deutschland – Waldflaeche konstant

[53] Henz, Patrick (2016): "Compliance is a Race Car."

2014: The Forest around Stone Mountain, Atlanta

Three years later, the musician and game designer Paul Norman created the computer game *"Forbidden Forest"*. Due to his background, as one of the first, he had been aware that not only gameplay and graphics are important, but also a fitting soundtrack. He created a game, as dark as The Cure's post-punk. In his forest, behind the numerous trees are appearing ghosts, skeletons and giant spiders. Another relevant picture, as inside the forest are awaiting risks and temptations, as language barriers, facilitation payments, bribery, demanding clients, smart competitors and even safety concerns. All factors to lure the individual further away from its path of virtue. Like in the *"Blair Witch"* project, the forest can be the end, as violations to FCPA (*"Foreign Corrupt Practices Act"*, the US Anti-Corruption Law) and other laws may directly lead into prison.

As the forest is important, we cannot replace our human employees with consciousness robots. We cannot use an *"Agent Orange"* what wipes out the psychological pressures, as this would target on the other side also ingenuity, creativity and integrity. Similar as in the tale of Hänsel and Gretel, the company, and especially its Ethics & Compliance department, must spread out crumbs of bread. If you abandoned the company path, it should be as easy as possible to get back. This can be reached by positioning the Compliance Officer as *"Trusted Advisor"*. Important is that a relevant level of trust exists that the employee knows that guideline violations based on accident, as missing knowledge, would be treated as an accident and not automatically lead to disciplinary sanctions. Furthermore, the focus should be on prevention, similar as in the second part of *"The Hobbit"* movie, employees must liberate their-selves from the daily tasks and climb up a tree to oversee the forest. Where no trees disturb the view, it is possible to understand the whole situation. With this information, the path and direction where to go is clear again and the forest can be left behind.

Patrick Henz

0000 1111 MODULAR COMPLIANCE

Corruption is no part of a culture, but a learnt behavior. Due to this, a global Compliance program needs a modular structure to address different risks and regional challenges. Thomas Jefferson, 3rd President of the United States, defined it like this: *"In matters of style, swim with the current; in matters of principle stand like a rock."* A global company or organization must and can demand from its employees that independent where they are in the world, they comply with laws, guidelines, vision and values.

1993 started a television-series, which should be break with former limitations and open the way for a new vision. Since the beginning, *"Babylon 5"* had been planned to run for five seasons, using a classic theater structure so that season 1 had been used as introduction and setting the stage, season 3 had been the climax with the epic battle between, what we thought, good against evil, and finally season five as the end of the play.

Being a space station deep in neutral space, Babylon 5 had been a melting-point for diverse cultures and alien species. Important that typical clichés as good and bad diminished, everybody acted in the grey area in-between; and with getting more information about the lead characters, the viewer achieved a better insight, *"nobody was who he or she seemed to be."* You even had empathy for the characters which could not get out of their skin, as you saw them running into their doom.

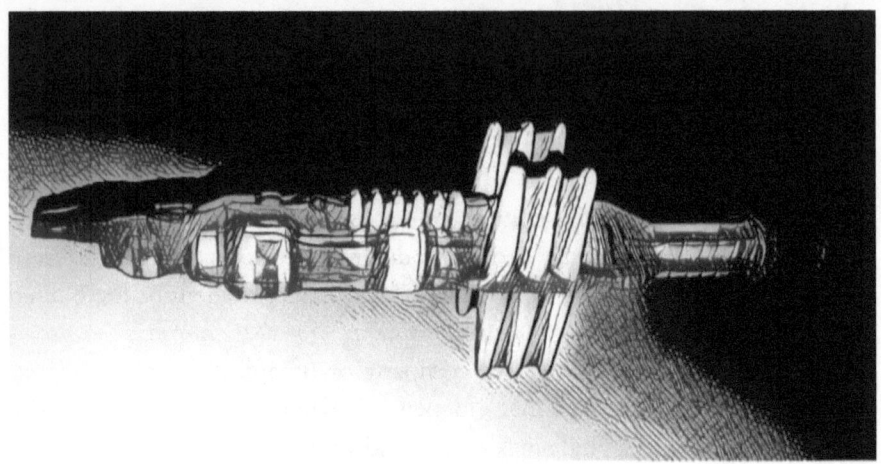

Babylon5

From an Ethics & Compliance point of view it was relevant to understand the different Alien species and their situation.

- **Centauri.** Even as their Empire had the best times already behind, they had been a proud species, which to the outside kept the appearance of old days. Behind the scenes families and groups fought about privileges and power. Due to this, the society became highly corrupted. Like many countries in today's Transparency International Corruption Perception Index.[54] Based on conflict of interest, the government does not always execute its own laws, an elevated level of impunity in the society is the result. For a global acting company or organization this is a risk factor, as their local employees may have learnt from early age on that facilitation payments and bribery may solve problems and thanks to general impunity no risks (law enforcement) are to be expected. Thanks to FCPA and UK Bribery Act, the company on the side, is not only responsible to potential non-effective local regulations, but also to the extra-territorial investigations of the US and UK Government (at their anti-corruption laws are ex-territorial). In its local trainings, the Compliance Officer must be clear that there is *"0 Tolerance for Corruption"* and that nobody inside the organization is above its

---

[54] Transparency International: Transparency International Corruption Perception Index 2015

guidelines. Due to today's globalization, especially younger employees know the situation in other countries. This can be taken as a Compliance Advantage and use trainings and communication not only to inform the employees, but motivate them for a change. This can be reached to foster their involvement by presenting them the relation between corrupt behavior and the economic growth of the region / social welfare. The cost of corruption is much more than the illegally paid sums, but the related loss of opportunities for the whole society.

- **Humans.** The democratic elected Earth-president lost his life in a mysterious accident and the vice-president came into charge. The beginning of a slow but steady removal of Democracy leads at the end to civil war. Indicators as *"The Economist Democracy Index"*[55] and the *"Reporters without Borders World Press Freedom Index"*[56] present a first overview of the country's political situation. A respectful, open and positive work culture is imperative for an effective Ethics & Compliance program, especially to implement an effective whistleblower-hotline. Employees have not only to believe that the company stays away from any kind of retaliation, but furthermore see reporting not as *"betrayal"* of the company, quite the opposite, it is an opportunity to support its sustainable growth.

- **Minbari.** The most advanced society of Babylon 5's main groups. Minbari act with principles, faith and logic. Classic corruption and bribery are non-existing. But this does not make them resist against ethical downfalls. If a group is based on values and principles, stress situations may lead to *"Ethical Blindness"*, a combination of different psychological pressures leads to a tunnel-view, where the individual is not able to see ethical traps, as he or she just focuses on the main-task. Ethical Blindness can lead to decisions, which are not compatible to individual and company values.

---

[55] The Economist (2017): "Democracy Index 2016"

[56] Reporters without Borders (2017): "2016 World Press Freedom Index"

- **Narn.** The Narn Regime just came out of the war, which destroyed large parts of its planet and infrastructure. Democracy must be learnt, and an Ethics & Compliance Officer can support in explaining the cost of corruption and its negative impact on the growth of a region. Not only from an economic point of view, but also freedom, democracy and justice.

Corruption is not part of a culture, but a learnt behavior. Due to this, it can be changed. Reviewing the four different situations, a company needs to establish a corporate behavior, which differs from the average in the region. With skills and knowledge such a task is achievable, as the organization and its members value the positive internal climate and protect it against the outside and possible rogue employees. Furthermore, this generalization should not mislead that cultural differences between offices in the same region could also be relevant. This as the corporate culture had been built up over years, based on the local management. Such difference between the company's locations must be handled with care, if not easily a resistance against any change will be built up.

0001 0000 TROUBLE WITH BUBBLES

We are living in *"post fact"* times. Thanks to the high number of information channels, it is impossible for the individual to check for all topics all available news channels. Mostly, people visit their favorite portals from which they assume that the published information confirms their own opinions. As result arise parallel societies, groups of people who life in the same region, but do not share the same information and attitudes. As perception is relative and the truth not given, but subject to interpretation. Due to psychological bias, the differences between the main groups get perceived as high, same as the similarities of the group members. This leads to the situation that trust levels inside the overall society are declining.

Corporations are aware of the different biases and thanks to their technological possibilities foster the bubble-effect. With the collected information about the use, social media portals present advertising from products, which had been visited earlier by the user and based on cross-selling statistics should fit. This maybe annoying, but critical it gets if not only advertising gets presented due to the user profile, but also news and information. So instead of linking to information what might challenge the individual's opinion or extend his or her knowledge, web-portals might link the user to the pages, which are confirming his or her existing opinion. This lets the person stay inside the comfort zone and keep him or her in calm and positive state of mind, needed for a successful shopping mood.

Thanks to the available information, the human individual transforms into a *"Lego Dimensions"*-figure. Here the little Lego figures include a chip, so that they can connect to a video console and if the sensor pad recognizes a figure, virtually the figure appears inside the game. Unlike a Cyborg most of humans do not have an implemented chip under their skin. Nevertheless, most of us a wearing a small device with what we could electronically identify ourselves: our smart phone. With the activated GPS, we are detectable, at least, if we do not deactivate this option. The internet will not stay limited to computer, tablets and smart phones. Thanks to the Internet of Things, everything will be connected. So imagine if you enter in the future your favorite fast-food restaurant, the soft drink dispenser will not start at the beginning to present all 200 potential options, but may recognize you and start with your five most bought drinks and maybe a new one what the company would like you to try. For the consumer an added value, but data privacy experts would warn that with based on this information, it will be easier to manipulate the individual.

Different social groups live in in their specific bubbles and opinions which criticize the bubble get declined or opposed. This is not only a social and political phenomenon, but also affects the corporate culture. A suspicious atmosphere counteracts an open and positive corporate culture. The last is important so that employees perceive the anonymous whistleblower hotline as choice. Using such a hotline always means stress and other psychological costs for the individual. If the person does not trust the company and that such a report would lead to a positive output, he or she would not use it.

On the other hand, increased individuals are communicators their-selves and broadcast via Twitter, Facebook, LinkedIn, YouTube, SnapChat or other channels. In the beginning of 2017, a lot of *"alternative"* or *"rogue"* Twitter accounts got created, where frustrated employees and members of official departments published their version of reality. Creating an anonymous social media account may need less than 5 minutes and is an easy and fast possibility to communicate to a high number of Internet users.

If the anticipated result of an internal whistleblower investigation is negative, meaning there is a high risk of impunity or even retaliation against the user of this hotline, and employee would not use it and instead stay silent to seek for other options to get his or her version of the truth get told. Due to many examples and the easiness to use Social Media, a possible anonymous account presents a risk for each company. It is management's responsibility to ensure a positive corporate culture. An Ethics & Compliance department should be position itself as figures of trust. The company must show 0 tolerance for retaliation and impunity!

0001 0001 Dark Matter – Dark Energy – Dark Net

Dark energy and matter are part of a theoretical model, as its existence could not be directly proved, but astronomical observations and calculations lead to the result that is must exist. Dark energy and energy are the solution to explain gravity between the galaxies and several other effects. Already Albert Einstein had the guess that the *"nothing"* between the objects is not *"nothing"*, but some kind of matter. Later the Hubble Telescopes confirmed this, as these unseen constructs would explain the current speed with what the universe continues to expand after the Big Bang.

Relevant for this model, the dark side is not the exception, but the rule. Based on calculations, the universe contains only 5% of ordinary matter, but 27% of dark matter and even 68% of dark energy, meaning that around 95% of the universe are non-direct measurable for us and the visible part makes up only around 5%.[57]

As common in mathematics, natural and artificial structures often develop alike. Also, the internet includes visible and non-visible parts. Besides the known net, surfed by the different browsers, where you enter an address or only name; or further surf via search-engines, there is another closed part. Accordingly, to astronomy there is a *"Dark Net"*. For this part of the web, there are no official names, but to connect, you must know a combination of numbers, it is not even possible to access such a site via its IP-address, as a used software anonymizes them. This code you can receive in chatrooms or other virtual hangouts. There is no possibility to receive it via a search engine. If you enter such Dark Net-sites, you may gain access to all kind of illegal content. This includes virtual one, as today's movies, stolen passwords, client databases and individual identities, but furthermore you may contact dealers for forbidden physical goods. Up to now, governments found not effective possibility to close the dark net and based on this

---

[57] NASA Science (fetched 11.03.2017): "Dark Energy, Dark Matter"

perception of anonymity and safety, it becomes slowly mainstream and more users access this part of the internet. A given treat to companies and society, as data cannot only easily be stolen, but with the dark net there is also a platform to sell this, only some clicks away.[58]

Luckily there is big different to the astronomical universe, the Dark Net only has an approximated seize of 3.4% of the open internet.[59] So it is not comparison to Dark Matter & Energy. There is another part of the net, the *"Deep Web"*. In opposite to the Dark Net, is this part of the internet not visible, as it is not catalogisized by a search-engine, but this does not mean that is content is forbidden or criminal. In fact, it is the opposite, most part of the Deep Web are extended data bases, as for example, from the NASA, the US National Climate Data Center or other libraries. Based on a 2001-study, the Deep Web is around 400 to 550 times bigger than the known public web.[60] Since then, recent studies are lacking, but we can assume that like Dark Matter & Energy, the Deep Web covers around 95% of the total internet. And it is expanding thanks to the Internet of Things. Today's and even more tomorrow's machines are real-time connected to the net and exchange information on a regular base. This communication will grow faster than the human social networks. But independent if human or machine communication, most of this information will be non-relevant.

Despite that the information is available, so it will be the task of smart people and software to make sense out of it and reduce it to create relevant analysis, statistical & causal relations and forecasts. This is a complex task, as statistical relations lead to causal interpretations. Doing so, the statistical relation may be misinterpreted, as other factors are excluded. And sometimes the mathematics only make sense, if we include a theoretical construct as Dark Matter and Dark Energy, even if we could not directly confirm its existence.

---

[58] Delamarter, Andrew (2016): "The Darknet: A Quick Introduction For Business Leaders"

[59] Howell O'Neill, Patrick (2015): "How big is Tor's Dark Net?"

[60] Bergman, Michael (2001): "The Deep Web: Surfacing Hidden Values"

0001 0010 A Playground for Compliance

For IT a *"playground"* is a separated part of the internal network or a single computer without network connectivity. This is required to test unknown or experimental software, what can include to study a new virus without having the risk to infect the organization's computers. Thanks to this, IT experts can understand the behavior of the software and whatever damage it could cause. The results are needed to update the anti-virus-protection.

A Compliance department can use this setup as a best practice. Today in most companies the Compliance controls, guidelines and tools are established. Luckily corrupt employees are rare, so in many cases the internal Compliance system never had to prove itself against a high-level violation. So how are we sure that it protects the organization?

Various companies hire *"White Hat Hackers"* , often on success fee. Their task is to hack the organization's computers and later inform the management how they did it. This to close safety leaks and make the protection more solid. A similar attempt can be taken by Compliance, external or semi-external resources can be used for a particular workshop. The task: *"How can I win a project with a bribe and not get caught by the internal controls?"* The participants could be student or interns. Internal employees might be problematic. They could be cautious not to create the impression that they know how to bypass internal processes, as they may fear to come up on the *"Compliance Radar"*.

The human brain is a super-computer, what includes the risk of getting hacked. This could be by integrated psychological effects (*"Ethical Blindness"*) or an external individual using social engineering. For this, the only protection is prevention. Internal workshops should include case-discussions or even role-plays to bring the employees into such a stress situation. In a relaxed atmosphere of a playground they take their role in the case discussion and are not afraid to produce crazy or potentially not-desired ideas. If a certain solution is learned for a similar example, the employee can activate this behavior in a stress situation and not depends on the search for a completely new solution, which under stress can easily lead to negative results for them-selves and or their organization.

Patrick Henz

0001 0011 THE RISE OF ELECTRIC CARS

A 4.6-meter-long executive sedan designed by Pininfarina and powered by an electric drive should be a worthy competitor for Tesla. But we are not talking about the *"next big thing"* from a known automobile manufacturer, but a *"fan made"*-project, an electric Alfa Romeo 164. An *"Alfisti"* converted this 1991 model from gas- to electric-drive.[61] With this, tt is the first Alfa Romeo e-car. But despite that the company's roots include electric vehicles. Before Alexandre Darracq founded with this Italian partner Ugo Stella A.L.F.A. ("Anonima Lombarda Fabbrica Automobili") in 1909, he already manufactured automobiles in his homeland France.[62] This included also the investment into electric cars, as for a short moment in time early pioneers thought that the electric engine would be the first mainstream solution. In 1895 inventor and GE co-founder Thomas Edison presented his first electric car proudly to press and public. Earlier, already in 1882, the Siemens and Halske company tested their electric model on a test track. In this case still not with on-board batteries, but using an overhead power line.[63]

But the development went for a long time into another direction. Nevertheless, Dieter Zetsche, Chairman at the Daimler Benz Board of Directors, mentioned at his visit of the 2017 *"South by Southwest"* (SXSW), for 30 years the leading conference for internet and pop culture that Tesla achieved to make electric cars sexy. Today consumers not only would consider buying an e-car because of its potentially positive impact on the environment, but because they are cool, fast and fun to drive. Of course, he mentioned Daimler's relation to Tesla, as the company supported them in their early years, also to financially stabilize them. Today the electric pioneer

---

[61] Berman, Bradley (2013): "Classic 1991 Alfa Romeo 164, Converted to Electric"

[62] Henz, Patrick (2017): "Italian Car Tales"

[63] Arbuckle, Alex (fetched 18.3.2017): "1880 – 1920 The first electric cars"

is a competitor, but also an inspiration. BMW already has two electric lifestyle products on the market, Daimler will follow until 2020.[64]

Back to Alfa Romeo. In 1976 the company presented together with the designer Bertone the concept-car *"Navajo"*. As a product of its time, it had been styled in actual futuristic lines. The minimalistic clear lines from earlier show-cars had been replaced by an opulent futuristic approach, including wings and plastic parts. What stayed had been the wedge. The silver color together with red line obviously reminded to science fiction movies. To foster this effect, Bertone even updated the Alfa Romeo logo and font set. The car still featured a known V8-engine, even if based on the design, you would expect a quit electric motor.

1976: Alfa Romeo 33 Navajo, 2.0L, V8, 2380hp & 8800rpm, design by Bertone

Today inside the Fiat Chrysler Company, Jeep and Alfa Romeo are positioned as the company's world brands, combining lifestyle, design and performance. Alfa Romeo is inside a re-launch, especially on the attractive US-market. New models as the Giulia and Stelvio are promising symbols for a bright future. We see that the brand is still strong in the automobile sector, convincing with Italian lifestyle and design. The available fuel engine completes this positive picture. But the market is changing, not only in the US, but also Europe and China. A powerful electric drive would fit and boost Alfa Romeo with an additional "coolness" factor. There is no question if the company will offer cars with electric or any other type of alternative drives, only when. A possible name to combine innovative technologies with the company's rich history is also available: *"Alfa Romeo*

---

[64] DRadio Eine Stunde Wissen – Was mit Medien (2017): "Smartphone – Das Über-Gerät"

Darracq".

Also, electric pioneer Siemens is again getting stronger involved into electric cars. In March 2017 the Swedish startup company *"Uniti"* announced that they raised over one million USD to market their concept of a compact electric vehicle. The idea is to sell this car later for around 22,000 USD. Due to the general attractiveness of the electric drive concept, Uniti could raise this sum from 570 different crowd-investors, mainly between 18-45 years and located in 45 different countries. This purely based on the idea, as no physical prototype exists so far. An ambitious project, where the borders between manufacturer and client are vanishing. One million dollar is, of course, a low budget if you plan to produce a car in Siemens designed fully automated factory, but new products and philosophies may lead to new business concepts. The raising possibilities of virtual reality need less traditional prototype testing.[65] Development costs could get lowered. A fully automated production line needs higher investment at the start, but in the production time itself, human costs, including salaries, but also income tax, are low. If Uniti can realize their idea, it will be a novel approach, which would mean a completely different work atmosphere, as the typical blue-collar positions would be reduced to a minimum and the company practically functions like an IT-company. To further reduce costs, inside a partnership Uniti would not need buying the factory, but other models are available. Instead of buying the production machines, the company could only pay for an agreed number of working hours, a leasing concept. Besides, new production possibilities as 3D-printing makes it easier for small companies to overcome economies of scale and compete with established competitors. Thanks to this, car manufacturing can go back to its roots, when building a car still meant craftsmen ship and the focus was on the artist to think of an attractive automobile.[66]

---

[65] Lambert, Fred (2017): "Crowdfunded electric car to be manufactured in fully automated factory desiged by Siemens"

[66] Henz, Patrick (2016): "Business Philosophy according to Enzo Ferrari"

2017: Uniti, press photo.

As electric cars are perceived as a lifestyle, it is understandable that Uniti, same as Tesla, has and want to offer the latest software, including an opportunity for self-driving.

0001 0100 ROBO ADVISORS & POKER PLAYERS

Robo advisors is a class of software what based on mathematical algorithms advise the bank's clients how to structure their financial portfolio. With this they replace human finance advisors. As known from business administration lectures, finance advisors are, strictly spoken, a contradiction, as if the bank employee would be to predict the future of the stock markets, he or she should not have to work anymore in the bank, but enjoy life thanks to the personal earnings.

Robo advisors can work on various levels. The intelligent software receives information about the company's financial results, performance and outlook. Based on this, the software can calculate the value of the company and decide if the shares at the stock markets are under- or over-valued.

There is a second approach. Besides this, human or robo advisors analyze the charts themselves to see if their short- or long-trends follow any potential lines or even break through such. This theory is based on mathematics, even if a causal relation is questionable. On the other hand, as individuals are following this theory and act so, as a *"self-fulfilling prophecy"*, positive results may or may not be measurable.

Besides all mathematics, pure psychology has a relevant impact on the development of shares. Individuals tend to invest into companies with a positive image, especially if they can involve the public into their portfolio. Psychology and financial results may contradict each other. It is the task of the financial advisors to interpret the information to decide if the shares will rise or fall.

Today we have a hybrid-situation, human and robo advisors are competing against each other, which also includes the competition of the different attempts, psychological interpretation against pure mathematical analysis. Important is that we are talking about advisors, human or not, they have no right to decide automatically in the name of the investor. If yes, especially robo advisors have the risk that their decisions may lead to financial catastrophes. If all bank houses have the same access to the information and the mathematical formulas come all to the same results that shares should be sold, the value of the affected companies may fall into bottomless. After such experiences, most governments implemented protections, including that stock markets could be temporary closed to avoid panic reactions.

In 2017, for a first time an Artificial Intelligence, called *"Libratus"*, won against human Poker-players.[67] Even more than in Chess, where humans already had been defeated before, Poker is based on rules and mathematics, but includes additionally a psychological component: *"bluffing"*. Due to the *"Massachusetts Institute of Technology"* (MIT), the game includes strategy, psychology and decision-making. Based on this understanding the prestigious university offers *"Poker Theory and Analytics"*, a course featuring eleven lectures.[68]

The free markets want to ensure that companies and organization have a fast and non-bureaucratic access to capital. To achieve that, investors also must have a non-bureaucratic choice to pull off their investments, to consume it or invest it into another, more promising company. Based on this concept potential successful companies can finance themselves and less fortunate organizations disappear from the market. In total, if company values include the potential sustainable results and investors do not search only for the *"quick win"*, the system means a general benefit for the society. But it is not a pure win-win-relation. Free markets create winners and on the side losers; victims. It is the responsibility of governments to ensure that all individuals have possibilities to benefit from the advantages, and that potential wins cannot go against losses by stakeholders, which not sit at the table. As today's projects must ensure sustainability, if not costs are paid by next generations.

---

[67] Solon, Olivia (2017): "Oh the humanity! Poker computer trounces humans in big step for AI"

[68] Colman, Dan (2015): "MIT's Introduction to Poker Theory: A Free Online Course"

To avoid stock markets, startup companies present their ideas directly to the public, this includes their visions, strategy and potential products and / or services. *"Crowdfunding"* is not only addressed to the classic investors, but also the potential clients, who share the vision and would like to see the potential products get reality. This method can be used for micro-investment, but also bigger projects. Often it is perceived as more than just a financial tool, as the name suggests, people are not only *"investing"*, they get emotionally involved with the idea and support to *"fund"* an organization. The requesters can be seen in the tradition of industry pioneers as Thomas Edison, Werner von Siemens, Yataro Iwasaki or Enzo Ferrari. All men, who saw their still young companies not only as a way to finance their living, but they had a vision that their products would chance the market to a better. Ethics lead to sustainability[69], and with this combination today's pioneers can convince to achieve the required financing via crowdfunding. To ensure that these platforms can continue with this claim, it is imperative that they get protected against potential fraud companies. Due diligences, background checks and an existing legal environment are imperative.

---

[69] Henz, Patrick (2016): "Let these visionary business leaders guide us to global sustainability"

0001 0101 ROBOTS AS AMBASSADORS FOR HUMANITY

Most likely, a first contact between our human civilization and a potentially existing alien life-form would not be done directly by an individual, but a robot. It could be that the Mars Curiosity Rover would find extra-terrestrial bacteria or that a higher developed species would read the greetings on the Viking-probes.

Artificial Intelligence and connected chat bots will be able to replace in many situations a human lawyer. With this they can be the first service level and only in a more complicated and / or less common situation, the case could be escalated to the human lawyer. With this, AI would replace human colleagues in companies, but on the other hand, could establish a first basic legal or medical support for groups, which up to today had no access to such support. The *"donotpay"*-project created such a robot lawyer.[70] Today the software can support for free if people look for compensation for delayed planes, help against unfair parking or speeding tickets. So far, the target group could be everybody inside the society. But thanks to relative cheap devices as basic smart phones or tablets, also more vulnerable groups could get support, for example related immigration questions or also healthcare checks.[71]

This example shows that a raising level of automation could support a re-humanization of society. Especially if the countries find a way to adapt to the raising automation level and could use the replaced employees for other relevant and challenging tasks.

---

[70] Do not Pay (fetched 20.03.2017)

[71] Brown, Jessica (2017): "The robot lawyer that helped people with their parking tickets is now helping refugees"

If the right humans are involved in the project, such uses could give hope and refute Albert Einstein, who once said: *"It has come quite appallingly obvious that our technology has exceeded our humanity."*

0001 0110 COMPLIANCE 2025

We are in a continuous technological revolution. Different experts predict that by 2025 30% of our today's jobs had been taken over by robots.[72] Already in 2016, the Knightscope K5 vigilance robot is patrolling autonomously in shopping centers. It is doing this with the costs of 6.26 USD/hour, much cheaper than a human.[73] If we think further, this means that in ten years also a machine could do the job of a Compliance Officer?

Artificial Intelligence is on the rise. Computer programs can crawl through required databases and the internet. For them it should be possible to search internal databases with the company's policies and guidelines, connect to external law databases and search the internet for news and actual interpretations of the law. Such results could be combined with other available databases, as for clients, payments and suppliers. With this a powerful software can answer all guideline- and law-related questions, even ensure a real-time monitoring of in- and out-going payments. Already today apps like Apple's Siri can communicate with a human-like voice, so that for the employee it will be hard to distinguish, if he or she speaks with a robot or human being. This software can connect to intranet, but also with the employee's laptops, tablet and smart phones. A 24/7-service is guaranteed. A related app can understand the employee's voice and process audio into information, further it can analyze the emotion in the voice, and understand if the employee is, for example, in a stress situation.

The 1912 born British mathematician and computer scientist Alan Turing helped during the Second World War to encrypt messages by the infamous Enigma machine. Ahead of his time, he saw computers and software not only as simple calculating machines, but as a base for artificial intelligence.

---

[72] Elkins, Kathleen (2015): "Experts predict robots will take over 30% of our jobs by 2025 – and white-collar jobs aren't immune"

[73] Vincent, James (2016): "Mall security bot knocks down toddler; breaks Asimov's first law of robotics."

"Cogito ergo sum" (Latin for *"I think, therefore I am"*) by the French philosopher, mathematician and scientist should be the relevant question to decide if a computer developed an IA or not. As thinking is a philosophical definition, he had to bring this on a practical level. The Swiss Psychologist Jean Piaget distinguished between 4 different phases and brought it to the point: *"Intelligence is what you use when you don't know what to do."*, so the inner process that the individual (human, animal or machine) starts, if there is no fitting script for the problem or situation.

To identify machine intelligence, Turing developed in 1950 the so-called Turing Test.[74] The idea is quite simple, different experts are communicating text-only with two players and must distinguish, who of them is a human being and who a machine. Up to today, machines had not been able to convince all the human judges, but results get better. In 2014 a chat-bot software portrayed a 13-year Ukrainian boy and with this could convince in the Turing Test 30% of judges, that it was a real boy.[75] IT companies assume that after the development of the smart-phone, intelligent chat-bots will be the next crucial step. Such software can connect to global databases, connect and interpret them.

For example, this software can reach out to global risk indices, as for example the Transparency International Corruption Perception[76], the Bribe Payers Index[77] and others. With this it ensures a real-time risk monitoring, what could replace the regular execution of different Compliance controls. Connecting risks, guidelines, employee's CV and travel activity, a software can go further and predict possible violations before the employee even think about it. Welcome to Philip K. Dick's world, as he described it already back in 1956 in his short story *"The Minority Report"*.[78] The algorithm of

---

[74] Turing, Alan (1950): "Computing Machinery and Intelligence"

[75] D'Orazio, Dante (2014): "Computer allegedly passes Turing Test for first time by convincing judges it is a 13-year-old boy"

[76] Transparency International (2015): "Corruption Perception Index 2015"

[77] Transparency International (2011): "2011 Bribe Payers Index"

[78] Dick, Philip K. (1956): "The Minority Report"

such a software would be based on Donald Cressey's Fraud Triangle and combine pressure, opportunity and rationalization.[79] This software will support the Compliance Officer, as his or her experience regarding human behavior and the company's business is required to calibrate the software and interpret its results.

1999: Spiralo

Even if we are still not there, it is the question, if this ever will be possible. The *"US Securities and Exchange Commission"* (SEC) already decided that a *"check-the-box"*-Compliance system is not sufficient to protect a company against Corruption.[80] The Compliance core function is not to inform employees about internal & external guidelines and execute efficient controls, but moreover to implement an adequate positive and sustainable

---

[79] Crassey, Donald (1973): "Other People's Money: A Study in the Social Psychology of Embesslement"

[80] U.S. Securities and Exchange Commission (2015): "SEC Charges BHP Billiton With Violating FCPA at Olympic Games"

corporate culture; Compliance is about humans. Still today the human brain is not completely explored, but for sure it is more complicated than today's existing computers, including the quite regular habit to act and or decide *"illogical"*. Further than that, the Compliance function needs to get perceived as a trusted advisor by the employees. To achieve trust, sympathy is a first step stone, and this often supported by similarities. A Compliance Officer can prove similarity with understanding of the business, learning local language, attending company events, etc. Similarity implicates that if you ask a question, the other person can understand it and is motivated to answer. A good start for the business relation. Of course, it is more required than sympathy and similarity, due to his or her expert knowledge, the Compliance Officer must find and give an adequate answer. Based on Compliance and business knowledge, the answer is tailor made for the requesting employee and not just a copy-and-paste from a standard database. For a complete non-physical software, it is difficult to establish such an atmosphere of trust, due to this, even the most intelligent software will not be able to replace a human Compliance Officer. But nevertheless, the modern technologies will bring new tasks:

- Modern technologies as home-office and 3D printing are reducing the economics of scale and opening small companies the possibility to act globally. Such startups are idea- and technology-driven, so that management is aware of products, services and how to sell this, but compliance-, legal- and export control-experience is lacking. The pro-active innovative technology philosophy may tempt the employees to take on risks, without being aware of the consequences.[81] The world is not becoming less complicated, the tendency is going to the other direction; a relevant risk, especially for small companies.

- Internet of Things. Even more than today, all machines and products will have a Wi-Fi-connection. This can be limited to a reading of information, but also lead to the possibility of a remote update of the machine's preferences and functions; with or without the end client's knowledge. Even without internet, machines

---

[81] See chapter 3.

can be programmed that way that they understand, when they are in daily-use or when they are in a test-, audit- or control-situation. With the IT-department, Compliance has a new target-group. Furthermore, an Internet of Things is vulnerable to cyber-attacks. In opposite to the Turing Test, it is not the machine, what must act like a human, but the human acting as a machine, or better said the human must create a software, which must react as another software. Here we not only talk about sophistic computers, but relatively simple machines, for example a printer. This machine is already today connected via the internet and can communicate with its manufacturer when new ink is needed. If the user bought a regarding service, the manufacturer sends the user the ink, when the printer indicates this. This machine does not have a complicated chip, so the online communication is simple. If a hacker can get inside this communication, he or she can with a software easily emulate the questions and answers of a printer. With such a hack, the manufacturer can get advised to send every week new ink to the user, or if the hacker additionally hacked the manufacturer database, new ink can be sent to his or her address, but billed to the original user.

- Millennials and following generations have a keen sense of ethics and see this as relevant for choosing a job. They are used to their independence and often do not want or can concentrate on just one task at a time. For this they need flexibility, but also a special approach to make them part of the work-team. As employers depend on these highly skilled experts, they must offer an attractive environment. Today life is more complicated, many employees expect more from their work than just money. They want to be satisfied with the output of their tasks, as their job should be a part of their life. Boundaries between private and business-life must vanish, private and company values must be compatible. The smaller the gap between these two values, the less the company must compensate a negative gap with higher salary. With this compliance and ethics show their value for the business, as employees want to be proud of the company that they are working for. Nevertheless, this is not a general advantage for Compliance;

personal ethics do not automatically have to be compatible with the law and company's guidelines. Further, these generations are not only raised with internet, tablets and smart phones, also they are used to Apps and media libraries, meaning they do not consume anymore linear television. Content is available, when the user wants to see it; it is not needed to wait for a special day and time. The disposition to wait is less developed than in earlier generations. Individuals and non-formal high technology groups may enforce ethics on their own. Data protection stays a relevant Compliance topic.

- Smartphones and wearables continuously collect information about their users, including which locations they are visiting, if they do this by car or walking. Such information could be interesting for the HR department, as based on this the health condition can be predicted and so future sick-times, especially if a central software not just could access these devices, but connects this information with central employee healthcare information database. Data privacy would be strongly violated. Wearables are only a small step away from William Gibson's vision of computer implants and cyber upgrades.[82] In fact, implanted microchips already today can enable blind people to see again, bionic parts replace lost arms and legs. In 2015 a group of hackers got the control of several cars; in future it would be theoretically possible to hack a human being. Cyborgs are a target for data privacy and cyber protection.

- Technical progress is not limited to wearables, also smart phones and tablets continue being a base for it. This as the user only must implement an app on the mobile device, which connects to the cloud or a single server. This is the place where the intelligent software is hosted, and the mobile device works primary as interface with the user. Due to this, an app is not limited on the technical possibilities of the device. Thanks to the microphones and cameras, next generation software can understand the emotional status of the user. This is relevant for Compliance, as a

---

[82] Gibson, William (1984): "Neuromancer"

calm person reacts different than a nervous one and for example, more vulnerable to develop ethical blindness. On the other hand, a too introvert person may be disinterested in Compliance topics, what is also not desired. If an intelligent software can distinguish not only between different situations and job positions, but also emotional status; information can be further tailor-made provided. Again, of course, this open concerns regarding data privacy. As the Cloud normally does not forget and the company may have statistics in which situations the employee lost his or her emotional comfort zone.

"Integrity is doing the right thing, even when no one is watching", said the Clive Stapes Lewis, novelist and poet from Northern Ireland. This defines that an Ethics and Compliance Department is about the Human Being and its psychology, observable as behavior. What about the scenario that robots and Artificial Intelligences join the workforce? Roboethics examines how human ethics can be used for robotics, including the development, manufacturing and use of robots. In 2014 hitchBOT hiked across Canada. To do so, scientist sat the little robot on the side of a highway with a message that it wants to travel and meet new friends. Then they tracked how drivers reacted to the machine. If they helped hitchBOT, ignored or even destroyed it. Even if there had been single bad experiences, the overall results had been quite promising.[83] Of course, its likeable design made it easy to like the little machine. Today scientists evaluate their results to see how much they can predict how in future humans will react to machines in their private or work environment. At least it can be said that there is no general aversion. Modern science fiction fosters this idea, as the droids R2D2 and C3PO are two of the most sympatric characters of the Star Wars saga. Further, in the 7th movie, director J.J. Abrams created one of the most emotional scenes, as Han Solo and Chewbacca find finally the Millennium Falcon. A spaceship without an intelligent board computer a la HAL, but nevertheless, the viewers connect this machine to their childhood adventures, so that it is perceived as a positive character.

---

[83] Hitchbot (fetched 10.6.2016)

The hitchBOT travelled through the US. Photo with friendly permission of hitchBOT.

This human-robot-interaction may lead on the other hand to another bias, the over-trust in the machine. People assume the robot or artificial intelligence must know best and furthermore takes the best decision, as the results are based on a detailed algorithm. A similar effect had been confirmed in 1961 Milgram experiment. Where participants executed the orders from a perceived scientist, even if these had been against own knowledge and values. In this setup of the experiment, the participants had been instructed to give a raising strength of electrical shock to a potential other participant. This other person sat in a different room and the participants had only audio contact. The participant had not known that this other person is part of the experiment team and, had been an actor and not received any shocks at all. With the raising strength of potential electric shocks, the actor simulated raising pain and requested to participant to stop. The potential leader of the experiment (the "scientist") ordered to give more shocks and many participants continued until the person from the other room stayed silent.[84] These results had been shocking, as it showed that how easy it may be to get individuals to obey, even if this would mean to hurt or even kill others. There had been later also critics to Milgram, as he let the participants to cross certain lines and showed them their inner abyss.

---

[84] Milgram, Stanley (1963): "Behavioral Study of Obedience"

Such an over-trust in the machine can be dangerous, especially in the scenario of an urgent evacuation, as humans may prefer to follow a robot, even if this is going in circles, instead to use their own knowledge of the building and leave as fast as possible.[85]

Artificial Intelligences, independent if they are part of a robot or just a software, have the possibility to learn by their-selves. Based on a database, they learn with new information and measurable trial and error. As even the most complex company guidelines cannot define all possible situations, an AI may come to the conclusions, that possible decisions may find the company in a grey area or even in violation to a law. A completely new situation for an Ethics & Compliance department, as similar for the human employees, it must focus to prevent and respond to AI wrong doings. The last can be registered, the same as any violation done by a human being. The difference is with the prevention. The human mind is a black box, based on decision making and social behavior theories we only can presume how an individual came to the shown behavior. In the case of a robot or AI it is different. If there is access to the software, it can be analyzed, and the behavior mathematically forecasted. If Compliance wants to keep its internal leadership for business ethics, it cannot limit this to human employees, but must be open to include in future also artificial ones in its scope.

We are in the process that software is taking over tasks, which today still are done by humans themselves. An example are self-driving cars, which most of the car manufacturers have on their to-do list. A raising individualism of the vehicles may disturb this development. As we have both trends, the question is, will it be necessary that each car would have to get an individual driving license, including a practical test, similar as each human driver must do? The first fatal accident of Tesla's autopilot had been explained by the company: *"Neither autopilot nor the driver noticed the white side of the tractor-trailer against a brightly lit sky, so the brakes was not applied."*[86] A problem which could

---

[85] Robinette, Paul / Li, Wenchen / Allen, Robert / Howard, Ayanna / Wagner, Alen (2016): "Overtrust of Robots in Emergency Evacuation Scenarios"

[86] Sivak, Michael / Schoettle, Brandon (2016): "A 16-Year-Old Needs a License. Shouldn't a Self-Driving Car?"

be electronically solved with updates on the software or mechanically on the camera. Similar as a person needs to advise for the getting or renewing the driver's license, if he or she needs glasses. In a next development step, the software can include Artificial Intelligence and learn from experience. This would lead to the situation that each autopilot would be different from another. Further mechanical parts, as for example camera lenses have wear-effects and for this, need regular maintenance and controls.

Even if the Tesla accident was a tragic event, it must be set into relation that 2013 in the USA died more than 32,000 people on the roads, which means 90 fatalities a day. All caused by human drivers.[87] Self-driving cars include assisted up to completely automated driving. In all cases human risks get replaced by computer risks. Due to today's statistics this reduces the overall risk, but not brings it to zero.

In opposite to other industries, in IT it is quite common to use the client as tester. Due to the competition, software developers release new apps, software and even operation systems, which are not fully tested and still are in a beta phase. Sometimes this is transparent for the user, sometimes not. Due to constant internet connection, this is less problematic than in other industries, as updates get downloaded and started before the user shuts the computer down or starts it a next time. The problem exists if a manufacturer offers both, hard- and software. Business culture cannot be changed as fast as it would be necessary. In 2016 Samsung had to recall its Galaxy Note 7 as the battery could start to burn. One result had been, that airlines explicitly asked Samsung Galaxy users to shut down their phones completely and not allowed the normal airplane mode. Employees of modern startups as Tesla and programmers of Self Driving software must be aware that they need to offer a product based on the NASA philosophy *"failure is not an option"*, as every software error may lead to human losses.

---

[87] Chen Aria Hangyu (2016): "U.S. has highest car crash death rate, despite progress, CDC says"

Even if luxury cars as Tesla are an important communication channel for the self-driving technology, a faster growth in the beginning could come from the commercial vehicles, where the *"pleasure of driving"* is no relevant factor. An intelligent software can replace the human driver and so take aware the risk that because of cost pressure drivers often are fatigue and cause related accidents. Furthermore, the self-driving vehicle will be included in the company's *"just in time production"*-process, so that speed and route could be adapted and with this the vehicle will arrive exactly at the time, when it is required to. This, of course, keeping in mind actual weather conditions and traffic situation. It is no surprise that McKinsey & Company forecasts that by 2025 already one third of the trucks will use advanced self-driving technology.[88]

As today's technologies give an impression for tomorrow's possibilities, the 2016 summer hit *"Pokémon Go"* is an interesting example. It was not the first augmented reality-game, for example the Star Wars app included already one year earlier a game, where the user can experience a Jedi training, where the drone appears in the real environment. But Pokémon Go was the title, what gave this technology the commercial break through. In short, the smart phone's camera is active, together with GPS localization and holding position on the phone, the software includes a virtual object into the video and the user can interact with this. An interesting technology, but still with a relevant problem. The user must take his or her eyes off the reality, but on to the screen of the phone or tablet. Augmented reality offers a non-direct perception.

Google introduced its *"Google Glass"* 2013 into the market. An electronic wearable in form of normal glasses, which included an optical display. The user could navigate through the screen via a touchpad on the side of the glass. Via different apps, the individual could use known software as maps, email, camera or video. Raising data privacy concerns let to an atmosphere that the society did not accepted single individuals to use Glass. Even

---

[88] O'Brien, Chris (2016): "One-Third of all Long Haul Trucks to be Semi-Autonomous by 2025"

violence against users had been reported.[89] Google reacted and took two years later the product from the market.

Nevertheless, it stays an interesting technology, especially if it could be connected with augmented technology. With this combination a user would not have to look on the screen of his or her smartphone to detect the Pokémon, but see it directly through the glasses. If further the glasses would be able to analyze the environment and know what the user is seeing, an app could react to the environment and the user; and so, include virtual reality. As known from science fiction movies as *"Minority Report"*. The individual could pass an electronic marketing area and each person would see a commercial which is based on his or her consumer preferences. No need to say that such a vision may be a nightmare for today's average human being. But there may be also more positive work-related uses, as a maintenance engineer may be accompanied by a virtual colleague with programmed inside knowledge about the client's installed base. Or inside a factory, a virtual warning may come up, if a safety procedure would be ignored. On the other hand, first studies came in 2016 to the result that such technology supports the development of a cognitive tunnel vision, as the Glass users focused more on the task, as the members of a second group, which used the same application (in this case Google Maps) on their smart phone. The study indicated that this combination of natural and virtual views fosters and excluding of natural environment, what means visuals and cognitive ideas[90]; a raising risk for ethical blindness.

Virtual and real world can merge, what would affect also the private life. There may be the situation that in an apartment is no more physical wall-clock, but augmented reality can project a virtual clock, every time the person is walking by. For this all kind of home applications as refrigerator, coffee machine or the oven could be connected to the cloud, but would not need having a physical display, as a virtual the glasses could create one. This allows the designers to create classic objects, without having the requirement to include a screen on the front. Two advantages, less

---

[89] Vazquez, Joe (2014): "Woman Wearing Google Glass Says She Was Attacked in San Francisco Bar"

[90] Hensel, Anna (2016): "Here's What 'Smart' Eyewear Does to Your Brain"

limitations for the design and lower costs, as physical displays can be replaced by virtual ones.

A potential second attempt for such intelligent glasses may come first in the work environment. If it would be successful there, it may enter the private life, too. But here a second development step would be necessary, such a wearable must be combined with a traditional glasses design; and ideally not to be distinguished by these. That way, social resistance may be overcome.[91]

---

[91] Henz, Patrick (2016): "Compliance is a Race Car."

Patrick Henz

0001 1000 THE CLOUD

Born in 1907, US author Robert A. Heinlein was part of the *"Golden Age of Science Fiction"*. He authored many novels and short stories, from which one became a movie adaption: *"Starship Troopers"*. Political interested, he had liberal thoughts and, typical for its time, was skeptical to group let decisions: *"A committee is the only known form of life with a hundred bellies and no brain."*

In opposite to a first thought that a decision taken by a group of people must be better than the decision, which was taken by an individual, group psychology indicates something different. Normally groups tend to polarize, due to this, decisions taken by a group are most likely more risky or radical, as the decision of just one person.[92] In most of the companies the time that one director or CEO was a sole decision maker passed away. Often for each decision applies a *"four-eyes"*-principle, accompanied by earlier approvals of the middle-management. Such a process wants to ensure that different experts can judge their decision from their point of view, but on the other hand opens a risk that managers approve without the required care as they know that others already have signed or still would sign.

One of Compliance key-messages is that every employee is fully responsible for his or her decisions, including signature and approval. A message which must be regularly fostered in trainings and communication. This is especially true for today, as virtual teams and cloud management become reality. Decision makers do know each other anymore in person, so become part of a virtual reality. Decisions here are perceived as less real as the ones, which we take in a personal meeting, this leads to the situation that also potential risks get perceived as less high, as if they would be discussed in an in-person meeting.

---

[92] Moscovici, Segre / Zavalloni Marisa (1969): "The group as polarizer of attitudes"

The Ethics or Compliance Officer is in many cases also responsible for Cyber Security, for this can counteract such risks. Similar risks are related to the usage of social networks, as users often are not enough aware that actions in the virtual reality can have real-life consequences.

Because of its size, the cloud is an ideal place to store Big Data. Thanks to the rising Internet of Things, where machines interchange information with each other and without a human user in-between, the world creates each day more data. In a business relation this opens the question, to whom belongs this information. To the client, the provider, both? As machines may be related to particular humans, for example in the healthcare sector, this question also is relevant for Data Privacy. Computer usage should not make it possible to identify an individual and allow assumptions about his habits, health or other situations. A sensible legal question, as different countries have different strict local laws. Local restrictions are limiting the cloud, as for all information apply the laws of the strictest participating country.

In future, the Internet of Things makes it even more imperative to define who is allowed to use the data, as intelligent software may use the big data to speed up the machine learning processes. As example, the manufacturer can sell its solutions to different companies and as the machines are all interconnected with each other, the cloud can learn from the products which are installed at the different clients A and B. Due to this, the manufacturer is learning from the installed machines at both clients and can offer e better solution to client C, even if it is a direct competitor for A and B.

Big Data should not be confused with Smart Data. Data itself is a collection of information and not includes any kind of intelligence. Only the connection of data with statistical methods and the possibility to predict future behavior or situations makes it smart.

This already presents the next problem; a statistical relevance does not automatically mean that we also have a logical relation. For example, a correlation coefficient may present a statistic relevant relation between A and B. This does not mean that A causes / influences B or the other way around. There may be the situation that A & B depend on an unknown factor C. If this is the case, there is not only a statistical relation between A and C, B and C, but also A and B. If C is unknown, a logical interpretation of A's relation to B may be completely wrong, even if this gets statistically confirmed. Of course, as often in astronomy, a scientist may conclude that even if there is a statistical relation, there is no logical one and due to this, an unknown factor C must exist. Further investigations may discover this later. An example had been Dark Matter. Scientists assumed that it exists due to behavior of the other factors, but could confirm this only decades later.

A problem of Big Data is that people have the temptation to use all of it, even it is not needed and / or does not bring an additional benefit, as a more precise forecast. Again, a critical tendency in relation to Data Privacy. If a company has sensible information, it is difficult to stop an organization to use it. Due to Donald Cressey's Fraud Triangle, it presents a high temptation as a company may get a more detailed insight of its employees or customers. This may lead to the promotion of employees with favorable health information or to a potential better understanding how to establish a more efficient communication or even manipulation of these individuals.

Lloyd of London estimated that cybercrime cost businesses up to 400 Billion USD a year,[93] for 2021 estimated the Herjavec Group already costs of 6 Trillion USD.[94] It is an on-going competition between hacker and organization, if the data is safe or not. Data protection is and will be relative. Due to this, a company should regularly review, which information should be stored, and which could be eliminated. Data which is not stored anymore, cannot get stolen and misused. This related it is important to remember that 60% of all attacks had been carried out by company insiders.[95] Such attacks can be on high- but also low-risk level; entering a virus from inside the system or just downloading the relevant information to an USB-stick.

---

[93] Gandel, Stephen (2015): "Lloyd's CEO: cyber attacks cost companies $400 Billion every year"

[94] Cybersecurity (2016): "Hackerpocalypse: A Cybercrine Revelation"

[95] Van Zadelhoff, Marc (2016): "The Biggest Cybersecurity Threats Are Inside Your Company"

Important, damage is not only caused by theft, but also data manipulation may lead to non-efficient processes. A relevant disadvantage in a competitive situation.

Again, for business or even politics, it is a high temptation to communicate a statistic relation between A and B, ignoring that an additional factor C exists. Such communication, against better knowledge, may lead to a manipulation of people. Here is not only true that a small percentage of people have access to such smart data, but like earlier media as books, radio and tv, most people use the internet for entertainment and not primarily to gain additional knowledge. So even if the tools are available to get smart data, a big part of the people do not use them and so are open for manipulation.

To avoid the misinterpretation of information, a company should analyze what data is really needed for storage and which not. Even if processes and guidelines limit the access to the data, there is always the risk of by-passing such access gates by internal employees, but also external hackers. In the movie Jurassic Park, the chaos theoretician Dr. Ian Malcom defined the risk: *"Life finds a way"*[96] . Like the dinosaurs, also information will find a way to break out of the protected cloud and end up in the hand of non-authorized employees, external hackers or the internet in general.

As data has the temptation to get used, virtual & physical is space available, there is a risk that data do not get removed after their license expired.

Big Data + Statistical Methods + Logical Theories = Smart Data

As discussed, methods and theories are imperative, but also a sufficient big pool of data, as without this the identified relations are not statistically significant. Or as the data scientist W. Edwards Deming said: *"Without data you're just another person with an opinion."*[97]

---

[96] Crichton, Michael (1990): "Jurassic Park"

[97] Henz, Patrick (2016): "Compliance is a Race Car."

0001 1000 HOW TO BRIBE A ROBOT

1) Corruption in the Age of Machine Learning

The robot, the perfect employee. No conflict of interest, all decisions based on information, rules and logic. The ideal vision for a Compliance Officer? Unfortunately, it is not that easy. A machine compliance today or in the near future is a rules-based compliance. Complete new circumstances may lead to a situation that none of the defined rules can apply. The machine has two possibilities:

1) Use the most similar known condition and apply its rules. This behavior opens the risk of the execution a wrong decision.

2) The software can decide that the situation is not decodable and stop its actions. Doing nothing, can also be the wrong decision.

2) Corruption is a Learnt Behavior

The case gets more complicated if we enter the gray zone between human and machine: Artificial Intelligence, the self-learning machine. Corruption is a learnt behavior. A software can learn positive behavior, but also non-desired one, if this is what leads to success.

Compliant and corrupt behavior are both learnt. This is important for machine learning, as the robot has no emotions, it bases its decisions purely on action and result. With an incredible speed the software can calculate the outcome with the most attractive result (possibility and value). Based on this, computers today are hardly beatable in board games as Chess or Go with limited choices (More complex situation are difficult to handle and may lead to wrong decisions, as the algorithm of a trading software let to 2010 to the stock market flash crash). Here they do not only calculate the best outcome for the actual move, but can calculate different scenarios for all probable future moves, keeping in mind all the opponent's possibilities. In a transparent country with effective anti-trust, -corruption or -money laundry laws, the software would come to the result, following the rules will promise the highest outcome. In a country with a high impunity index, the machine may come to a different result. Following laws will create a lower potential output as bypassing them. This based on the calculations that the risk of getting caught by law-enforcement is minimal. Such a result should get fostered, if the machine works with Isaac Asimov's

Three Laws of Robotics:

1. *"A robot may not injure a human being or, through inaction, allow a human being to come to harm.*
2. *A robot must obey the orders given it by human beings except where such orders would conflict with the First Law.*
3. *A robot must protect its own existence as long as such protection does not conflict with the First or Second Laws."*[98]

As all business decisions may lead to the situation that single individuals come to harm, for example, lose their source of income based on a required job-cut, Asimov himself identified the need to add a fourth or zeroth law to the original ones:

"0. A robot may not harm humanity, or, by inaction, allow humanity to come to harm."

As corruption is no crime without victims and causes related costs for the victims, an intelligent machine or robot would have avoided any corruption. As addressed in many science fiction books and movies, on the other hand this may cause that the machine decided to protect humanity against itself and prohibit the free will.

---

[98] Asimov, Isaac (1950): "I, Robot"

The quality of the software, with other words, the teacher is important. In March 2016 Microsoft launched its artificial intelligence „Tay", a chat-bot which should be able to friendly chat with internet users via Twitter and Facebook. To do so, Tay learnt from these talking partners. An exciting experiment, which went completely wrong, so that Microsoft hat to shut down the software less than 24 hours later. What happened? A certain group of users took advantage of the Tay's innocence. Even as the software was highly intelligent, it started with no experience, like a baby. Organized users taught Tay radical political positions, so that the software learnt this and started to copy its teachers and communicated these statements of hate. The experiment showed a disturbing similarity to the Stanford-Prison-Experiment, which also had to be ended before its planned time.

Even if the country has a high impunity level, other factors must be included. If compliance with the law would not get enforced, corruption would destroy the market, as the final cost of corruption is the destabilization of the region and rise of radical political parties to replace former conservative ones. In average, this will not lead to combat corruption, but its perfection and a further economic downturn, including the country's education, art, culture and social life.

A modern company's Compliance system works with values and controls, Asimov's Law[99] provides the basic fixed values for a robot or intelligent software. Like a Compliance system we cannot keep the machine alone with this. Artificial Intelligent researcher and author Andrew Rosenblum created the example that the self-driving car faces the situation that a truck is approaching from the front, what surely will destroy the car and kill its passenger. The only possibility to avoid this situation is to swerve and drive the car into a group of 15 pedestrian. Purely based on Asimov's Law, the car would have to do the mathematics and decide to sacrifice its own passenger. This may interfere with the car's obligation to protect its passengers and owner.[100] Due to this, the car manufacturer may feel tempted to include an additional guideline into the software that the car has to protected its owner, as this is the person who pays the company for the intelligent car. What about the 1:1 situation, where the decision is to sacrifice the passenger or one pedestrian? Here the car must decide always in favor of its passenger? A government cannot burden such a decision on the car manufacturer, programmer or the software. It must establish laws and guidelines, which an Intelligent Software must follow, especially in such grey areas. If such a near future scenario, the Compliance Officer must be able to control the potential "if-then"-strings of the software. As the discussion about the Volkswagen defeat-software and emission controls show, software engineers are under high pressure to reach the high external and internal goals; they are tempted to find solutions to bypass the regarding controls.

---

[99] Asimov, Isaac (1950): "I, Robot"
[100] Rosenblum, Andrew (2016): "Fully Autonomous Cars are Unlikely, Says America's Top Transportation Safety Officer"

2016: Alfa Romeo Giulietta

Today chip-tuning is already used to change the management of the engine and find additional horsepower. This is in most cases legal, but liberates the car manufacturer from its guarantee. When self-driving cars are a relevant market, it is a question of time, when programmers will offer software to ensure a higher safety for their owners, programmed preference for the passenger against the pedestrians. As different countries have different legal-systems and underlying values, for example Roman or Anglo-Saxon Law. Most properly an autopilot requires different processes for such decision making. In one country choosing the option with the less numbers of victims maybe be adequate, but in another country actively driving the car against this one person may be interpreted as an active act of killing and murder. The German Government installed a commission to elaborate ethics rules for self-driving car. The regulators stated that *"age, sex or physical condition of any people involved"* should not determine the decision if an accident is unavoidable.[101]

A human driver instinctively may try to protect the baby and could as reflex, drive the car against a senior person. In this case, there the result is not based on an extended decision-making process, so there was no need so far to discuss the ethical aspect of the situation. In opposite to this, an autonomous car is acting on clear rules. The decision to prefer the baby

---

[101] Loewenberg, Gabriel (2017): "Germany Drafts Ethics Rules for Self-Driving Cars"

against the senior person would have to be programmed right from the beginning and in the particular situation the car follows such a script. Of course, human drivers may also take the cognitive decision whom to prefer in such situation, but nevertheless there is no automated script and there maybe never taken such decision and the individual is forced to face the scenario with no direct script to use.

Or what about an accident between an autonomous car with a traditional one? Due to potential higher risk of failing, the human driver from the beginning must defend him- or her-self to not automatically getting judged as the causer of the accident?

Governments and car manufacturers are required to find solutions how to avoid such chip-tuning, via law, but also technical protections against non-approved software. Like today's computer viruses, it will be a continuous competition between new viruses and the anti-virus industry.

3) Perception is subjective

- Gifts, Hospitality and Entertainment can distract a human being and lead consciously or sub-consciously to a wrong and psychological influenced decision. An individual cannot divide perception from interpretation. Originally, the human eye sees everything upside down, but in its first days, a baby learns automatically to re-interpret this, so that we „see" everything as it is, what is up, we see up and what is down, we see down. As the human brain tries to facilitate the execution of information, processes get simplified, we „think in drawers" and perceive similarities more similar than they are and the differences as more different.

- With a machine this is not possible, so perception must be altered directly. Perception is subjective, a robot needs a database to interpret a picture, similar to Google Goggles. An IT specialist or Hacker could alternate the database, so that the machine does not recognize the seen or changes its interpretation.

- We are on the edge getting Cyborgs. Already today small implemented microchips can support blind people to see again. Today piercings and tattoos lead to individualism, in future we may also „technically upgrade" our senses and muscles. Such minicomputers open the theoretical possibility to hack a human being. Let him or her see different pictures or even manipulate feelings. Already today exist brain implants for deep brain stimulation (DBD). This stimulator is used to treat the Parkinson' disease, but also depression other chronic pains. Via a small wireless antenna, the doctor can access and control the implant. Such a wireless control over the brain could be a target of a hacker attack. With such an uncontrolled access, the brain could be practically hi-jacked. An expert hacker could stimulate various parts of the brain und induce extreme behavioral changes.[102]

From an ethical point of view, a not to be estimated risk-factor. US and Chinese students claimed at the 2016 Defcon conference that they hacked a Tesla S model, in particular its autopilot sensors. With this hack it was possible to the group to take off another car from the Tesla's sensors and with this to make it invisible for the car's autopilot. If executed in a real environment, this can lead to an accident of the blind car.[103] Since the announcement and the later introduction of its cars, Tesla is in the international spotlight. This is also fostered by its famous founder Elon Tusk, as this gives the products an emotional component and so a unique selling proposition, difficult to get copied by the established car industry. As the management is aware of this prominent position, it knows that Tesla with all its connected high tech is favored target for global hackers. Company and cars have the latest protection against cyber intruders. If we can assume that if it was possible for cyber intruders to bypass such protections, even more probable it is that hackers could enter an industrial robot or intelligent office software, as many of these products had been developed by medium size companies and often include public open-source software in their codes.[104]

---

[102] Pycroft, Laurie (2016): "The latest cyber security threat? Brainjacking"

[103] Greenberg, Andy (2016): "Hackers fool Tesla S's autopilot to hide and spoof obstacles"

[104] Henz, Patrick (2016): "Compliance is a Race Car."

0001 1001 SWARM INTELIGENCE, NEW COMPLIANCE RISKS

Independent from the elements exists swarm behavior. It could be a group of birds, zebras or fishes. A complex number of individuals move as one, this is not only effective, but also beautiful for the observer's eye. An ideal what scientists want to use as example to improve the decision-making process. Internet, especially Clouds, have the possibility to connect individuals, artificial and human ones. A person stays connected to his or her group, this could be his team, but also a network of experts.

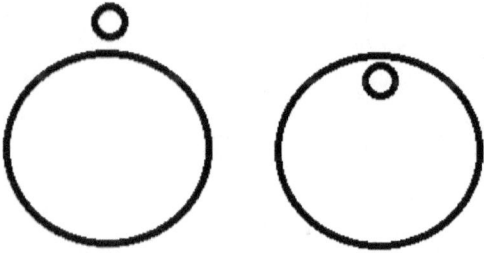

Modern companies support a *"democratization of management-style"*. Unlike in the past, managers should not be above the teams, but on top of them, still inside the group. Team members are encouraged to address their comments to their manager, even if this includes a contrary opinion. Less autocratic management-styles lead to a more positive work atmosphere and allow the leader to include additional experience into his or her decision-making process. With this the leader is easier to control and violations to company guidelines mean according disciplinary sanctions. Managers who are above the rules is a problem of the past.

This planned change can lead to new ethics & compliance risks. Being above the group, the manager was protected against group-pressure effects. The modern leader is still part of the group; accordingly, group-pressures can affect them. A study by the *"Vanderbild University's Owen Graduate School of Management"* concluded that even high-ranking executives may violate laws and guidelines, if they perceive this as the best for the group. The likelihood raises, if the manager strongly identifies with the group.[105] Even if not pressured into violations of guidelines, there is a permanent pressure that the group pushes individuals from the edges back to the center of gravity. High performers may get demotivated by the potential passivity of his / her co-workers and so thrown down to become an average performer.

The risk is identified, so it is up to the company to prepare their employees. Management trainings shall not teach only soft and hard skills, but furthermore present the different psychological pressures. Awareness is the first step of protection. Different exercises can support the required pressure relief.

Swarm Intelligence, Cloud and Internet support the connection to groups, including human and virtual members. As networks get smarter, it is up to the company to make its employees smarter too.

Psychological pressures can be overcome, if we take out personality and anonymize the participants of the group. Traditional online-panels, often used by market research companies, had been taken to a next level by the company "Unanimous A.I."[106], which developed an app, where a selected online community can answer, without discussion, different multiply-choice questions. The participants answer independently the questions and computer presents the real time results like a classic Ouija board, where in a séance a group of people try to contact the spirit of the death. The number of the participants' answers move the "planchette" to the edges of the board, where in this version are no letters, but the different multiply choice answers. If a sufficient number of answers magnetic-like moved the planchette over the answer, the AI takes this as the group's answer.

These graphic similarities maybe are no coincidence, as to avoid psychological group pressure, the participants are anonymous and

---

[105] Dishman, Lydia (2017): "Why Becoming A Leader Makes Some People More Unethical"

[106] Unanimous A.I. (fetched 05.10.2017)

unreachable, just as ghosts. In his novel "The Minority Report"[107], author Philip K. Dick presented a society which produced a limited number of individuals with the ability to see fragments of the future. As these visions had not been always adequate, to validate correctness of the information, at least two from three "precogs" had to have the same vision. A special police department used the precogs to previsualize future crimes and arrest the future murders before they can execute the crime. Like the movie, the participants of the virtual group are precious, and must be protected to avoid contact with lobbyists and other interested groups. In opposite to the Minority Report, there are no general mutants with the ability to see the future, but each topic requires a different group of interested participants. Artificial Intelligence and statistic formulas ensure that the participants are independent from each other, not only in relations, but also in character, knowledge and attitudes. With this, Unanimous A.I. achieved positive results via cognitive guessing by the single participants and predicted the results from horse racing or Oscar events. Based on this concept, Swarm Intelligence" or "Hive Mind" has one significant difference to natural swarms, they do not include all participants of total population, but only a small interested part, for every prediction parted into new groups.

This idea can be used for the corporate decisions making process. In traditional processes, such is done on a functional level and later, higher levels must approve the potential decision. This setup is time-consuming and may lead to a "bystander effect". The higher approvers see the earlier, physical or electronic, signatures and trust that these employees already checked the topic, especially as they are the experts on the topic. Due to this, not all approval steps foster the quality of the decision. In Philip K. Dick's novel, the precogs stayed inside a dark water-tank. Such devices exist since 1954 and should elaborate a relaxing atmosphere, where individuals completely separate their-selves from the environment. Sensory Deprivation Tanks reduce or suppress gravity, sight and sound. The neuropsychiatrist John C. Lilly experimented with his first Isolation Tank and hoped to create LSD-like experiences for the users. With the absence of any external stimulation, the human brain should be free to listen to

---

[107] Dick, Philip K. (1956): "The Minority Report"

potential internal stimulation. Even if this could not get reached, the devices are nevertheless still used today for chronic pain, hypertension or muscle tension treatments.

Unanimous A.I.'s approach shows that the tanks might not be necessary. A company may implement an internal group (not a think-thank, as the members are only voting, but not discussing) to decide about different non-daily topics. As group decisions tend to be more risky than individual ones, such a hive-result still requires confirmation by a higher management level. This setup does not only cut down the time for decision making, furthermore it ensures that all involved parts must think for their-selves, as they could not rely on earlier approvals. It ensures a higher quality of the decision-making process.

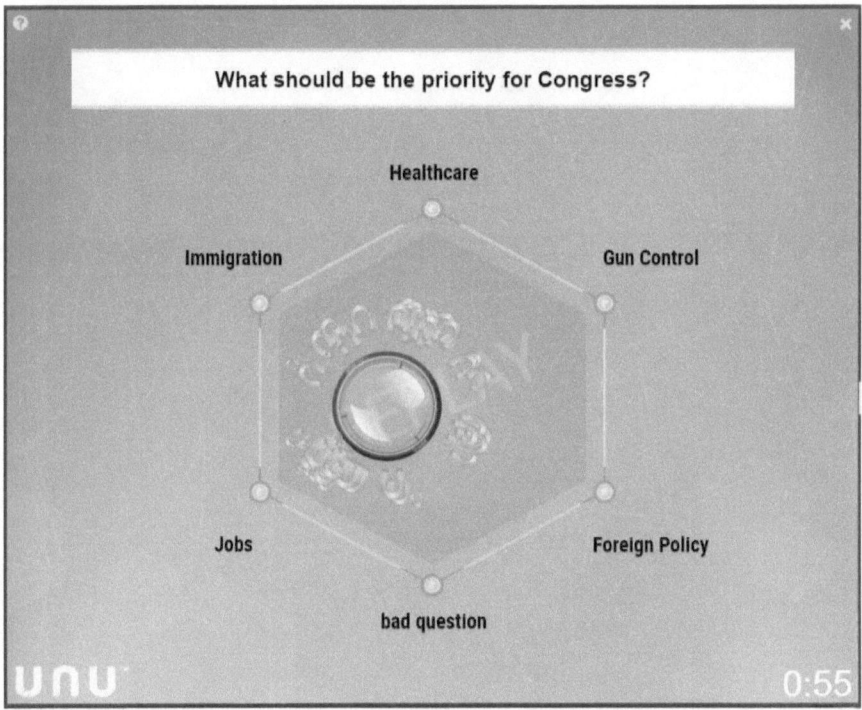
Swarm Insight. Photo with friendly permission of Unanimous A.I.

Swarm Intelligence is highly compatible with the concepts of Edward

Deming, who understood companies as complex processes.[108] Using the idea of the Hive Mind, knowledge not needs to be concentrated at top management and headquarters, but instead of this builds up and distributes over the whole local or global organization. Important predictions are not made in departments, but by virtual project groups. Thanks to this, the company can implement slim structures, as less static expert groups are required. To avoid psychological pressures, the Swarm Intelligence gets used for the prediction, management stay with its responsibility to take decisions. The Hive Mind is not geographically located, but understandable as a Cloud. Due to this, it supports an approach, where a classic headquarter is not requires anymore, but instead centers of competence pop up, where knowledge naturally gets together, for example based on the requirements of local markets or the contact with a relevant university. Such centers of competence take on global responsibility.

---

[108] Deming, William Edwards (2000): "The New Economics for Industry, Governance, Education"

Z CONCLUSION: COMPUTERS ARE USELESS

In an interview from 1964, the Spanish painter Pablo Picasso had been asked about his opinion regarding mechanical brains and calculating machines; this as the term *"computer"* was not prevailed yet. Picasso replied that they had been useless as they only can give you answers.[109] These words had been spoken more than 50 years ago, nevertheless they stayed valid despite the discussed technical progress. Machines still stayed machines and companies and organizations are around humans; their skills, requirements and dreams. If there is no goal defined, efficient processes cannot lead to such.

On the other hand, Artificial Intelligence and robots can take off workload from us and 3D printing and Virtual Reality even reduce investments and testing time. Humans which can to adapt to the modern times, are able, thanks to the technology, to concentrate on humans and their requirements. Nevertheless, this would be no automatic development, but requires a positive change atmosphere and prepared governments. It is in our hands.

---

[109] Fifield, William (1964): "Pablo Picasso: A Composite Interview"

Welcome to "ACCESS GRANTED – Tomorrow's Business Ethics Vol.2"! In a classic sense you have science fiction in your hands, as the book analyzes today's developments, as artificial intelligence, internet of things, predictions, deep learning, smart data, virtual twins and augmented reality, to discuss to which potential tomorrow's scenarios, including ethical dilemmas, they may lead. The different chapters provide answers, and at the same time give the reader new questions to think about.

As with all good science fiction, tomorrow's visions are in this or another way already relevant for today. This also as at the end, human- and machine-learning & -behavior is not that different. Today and even more tomorrow, humans and machines will work together to achieve the best possible results. This requires that both act based on the same values and attitudes.

1.edition, 156 pages. ISBN: 1979899487, ISBN-13: 978-1979899482

0000 0000 BIBLIOGRAPHY

- Arbuckle, Alex (fetched 18.3.2017): "1880 – 1920 The first electric cars": http://mashable.com/2015/07/20/early-electric-cars/
- Bader, Daniel (2016): "How to use Prisma for Android": http://www.androidcentral.com/prisma
- Beagle, Peter (1968): "The Last Unicorn"
- Bergman, Michael (2001): "The Deep Web: Surfacing Hidden Values": http://quod.lib.umich.edu/cgi/t/text/text-idx?c=jep;view=text;rgn=main;idno=3336451.0007.104
- Berman, Avis (fetched 14.01.2017): "Roy Lichtenstein Foundation – Biography": http://lichtensteinfoundation.org/biography/
- Berman, Bradley (2013): "Classic 1991 Alfa Romeo 164, Converted to Electric": http://www.ebay.com/motors/blog/classic-1991-alfa-romeo-164-converted-to-electric/
- Bostrom, Nick (2003): „Are you living in a computer simulation?": https://www.simulation-argument.com/simulation.html
- Brandon, John (2016): "6 Amazing A.I. Tricks in Microsoft Office That Make You More Productive": http://www.inc.com/john-brandon/6-amazing-ai-tricks-in-microsoft-office-that-will-make-you-more-productive.html
- Brown, Jessica (2017): "The robot lawyer that helped people with their parking tickets is now helping refugees": https://www.indy100.com/article/robot-lawyer-parking-tickets-helping-refugees-donotpay-chat-bot-7623241
- Bundesministerium für Ernährung für Landwirtschaft (fetched 24.2.2017): Waldland Deutschland – Waldflaeche konstant: https://www.bundeswaldinventur.de/index.php?id=710
- Cain, Frasier (2017): "We are Living in a Simulation?": https://www.universetoday.com/130704/are-we-living-in-a-simulation/
- Colman, Dan (2015): "MIT's Introduction to Poker Theory: A Free Online Course": http://www.openculture.com/2015/07/mits-introduction-to-poker-theory.html
- Crichton, Michael (1990): "Jurassic Park"
- Delamarter, Andrew (2016): "The Darknet: A Quick Introduction For Business Leaders": https://hbr.org/2016/12/the-darknet-a-quick-introduction-for-business-leaders
- Dick, Philip K. (1956): "The Minority Report"
- Dick, Philip K. (1968): "Do Androids Dream of Electric Sheep?"
- Dishman, Lydia (2017): "Why Becoming A Leader Makes Some People More Unethical": https://www.fastcompany.com/3068385/why-becoming-a-leader-makes-some-people-more-unethical?platform=hootsuite
- Do not Pay (fetched 20.03.2017): http://www.donotpay.co.uk/signup.php
- DRadio Eine Stunde Wissen – Was mit Medien (2017): "Smartphone – Das Über-Gerät"
- Elkins, Kathleen (2015): "Experts predict robots will take over 30% of our jobs by 2025 – and white-collar jobs aren't immune": http://www.businessinsider.com/experts-predict-that-one-third-of-jobs-will-be-replaced-by-robots-2015-5
- European Parliament Research Service Blog (2017): „Have Your Say On Robotics And Artificial Intelligence!": https://epthinktank.eu/2017/02/07/have-your-say-on-robotics-and-artificial-intelligence/
- European Union (2016): "Draft Report with recommendations to the Commission on Civil Law Rules on Robotics": http://www.europarl.europa.eu/sides/getDoc.do?pubRef=-//EP//NONSGML%2BCOMPARL%2BPE-582.443%2B01%2BDOC%2BPDF%2BV0//EN

- FAT/ML (2017): "Principles for Accountable Algorithms and a Social Impact Statement for Algorithms": http://www.fatml.org/resources/principles-for-accountable-algorithms#social-impact
- Ferrari.com (2016): "Scuderia Ferrari All Access – The Team opens up to fans": http://formula1.ferrari.com/en/scuderia-ferrari-all-access-the-team-opens-up-to-fans/
- Festinger, Leon (1957): „A Theory of Cognitive Dissonance"
- Fifield, William (1964): "Pablo Picasso: A Composite Interview"
- Fischer, Lorenz / Wiswede, Guenter (1997): „Grundlagen der Sozialpsychologie"
- Futurism (2017): "Our Computers Are Learning How To Code Themselves": http://futurism.stfi.re/4-our-computers-are-learning-how-to-code-themselves/
- Galeon, Dom / Marquart, Sarah (2016): "Finland isn't alone in trialing a universal basic income, Canada is trying it as well": https://www.weforum.org/agenda/2016/11/can-a-universal-basic-income-work-another-country-is-giving-it-a-go?utm_content=buffer7bca4&utm_medium=social&utm_source=twitter.com&utm_campaign=buffer
- Global Entrepreneurship and Development Institute: "Global Entrepreneurship Index 2017": https://thegedi.org/global-entrepreneurship-and-development-index/
- Griffin, Matthew (2017): "Robots to get legal recognition as Europe vots to classify tem as 'Electronic persons': http://www.globalfuturist.org/2017/01/robots-to-get-legal-recognition-as-europe-votes-to-classify-them-as-electronic-persons/
- Grut-Williams, Oscar (2016): "Robots will steal your job: How AI could increase unemployment and inequality": http://www.businessinsider.com/robots-will-steal-your-job-citi-ai-increase-unemployment-inequality-2016-2?r=UK&IR=T
- Henz, Patrick (2016): "Business Philosophy according to Enzo Ferrari"
- Henz, Patrick (2016): "Compliance is a Race Car."
- Henz, Patrick (2016): "Let these visionary business leaders guide us to global sustainability": http://www.tradeready.ca/2016/global_trade_tales/let-visionary-business-leaders-guide-us-global-sustainability/
- Henz, Patrick (2017): "Italian Car Tales"
- Hern, Alex (2016): „Elon Musk: ‚Chances are we'll living in a simulation': https://www.theguardian.com/technology/2016/jun/02/elon-musk-tesla-space-x-paypal-hyperloop-simulation
- Howell O'Neill, Patrick (2015): "How big is Tor's Dark Net?": https://www.dailydot.com/layer8/tor-dark-net-study-size/
- Junge, Christine / MacDonald, Ann (2011): "Therapy dog offers stress relief at work": http://www.health.harvard.edu/blog/therapy-dog-offers-stress-relief-at-work-201107223111
- Internet World Stats (fetched 14.03.2017): "Internet Usage Statistics": http://www.internetworldstats.com/stats.htm
- Knight, Will (2017): "Andrew NG Has a Chat-bot That Can Help with Depression": https://www.technologyreview.com/s/609142/andrew-ng-has-a-chat-bot-that-can-help-with-depression/
- Lambert, Fred (2017): "Crowdfunded electric car to be manufactured in fully automated factory desiged by Siemens": https://electrek.co/2017/03/16/electric-car-fully-automated-factory-siemens/
- Lee, Aileen (2013): "Welcome to the Unicorn Club: Learning from Billion-Dollar Startups": https://techcrunch.com/2013/11/02/welcome-to-the-unicorn-club/
- Livni, Ephrat (2017): You next lawyer could be a machine": https://www.weforum.org/agenda/2017/02/machines-could-soon-replace-lawyers
- Loewenberg, Gabriel (2017): "Germany Drafts Ethics Rules for Self-Driving Cars": http://www.thedrive.com/sheetmetal/13746/germany-drafts-ethics-rules-for-self-

- driving-cars?xid=twittershare
- MacDonald, Cheyenne / Best, Shivali (2016): "Dubai police launch AI that can spot crimes BEFORE they happen": http://www.dailymail.stfi.re/sciencetech/article-4062936/Dubai-police-launch-AI-spot-crimes-happen-Crime-Prediction-software-identifies-patterns-human-miss.html?sf=pygwkwa#ab
- Moskowitz, Clara (2016): „Are We Living in a Computer Simulation?": https://www.scientificamerican.com/article/are-we-living-in-a-computer-simulation/
- Maslow, Abraham (1943): "A Theory of Human Motivation"
- McLaughlin, Eliot (2017): "Suspect OKs Amazon to hand over Echo recordings in murder case": http://www.cnn.com/2017/03/07/tech/amazon-echo-alexa-bentonville-arkansas-murder-case/index.html?sr=twCNN030717amazon-echo-alexa-bentonville-arkansas-murder-case1004PMVODtopLink&linkId=35217286
- Mellino, Cole (2016): "The World's Largest Earth Science
- Experiment: Biosphere 2": http://www.ecowatch.com/the-worlds-largest-earth-science-experiment-biosphere-2-1882107636.html
- Metz, Cade (2013): "8 Years Later, Google's Book Scanning Crusade ruled 'Fair Use'": https://www.wired.com/2013/11/google-2/
- NASA Science (fetched 11.03.2017): "Dark Energy, Dark Matter": https://science.nasa.gov/astrophysics/focus-areas/what-is-dark-energy/
- Palazzo, Guido / Krings, Franciska / Hoffrage, Ulrich (2012): "Ethical Blindness"
- Park, Denise C. / Huang, Chih-Mao (2010): "Culture Wires the Brain: A Cognitive Neuroscience Perspective": https://www.ncbi.nlm.nih.gov/pmc/articles/PMC3409833/
- Poe, Edgar Allan (1839): "The Man That Was Used Up"
- Price, Rob (2016): "Stephen Hawking: This will be the impact of automation and I on jobs"
- Prisma Labs, Inc. (2016): "Terms of Use": http://prisma-ai.com/terms
- Quito, Anne (2016): "Sixth Sense – This woman, a self-described cyborg, can sense every earthquake in real time.": https://qz.com/677218/this-woman-a-self-described-cyborg-can-sense-every-earthquake-in-real-time/
- Reporters without Borders (2017): "2016 World Press Freedom Index": https://rsf.org/en/ranking
- Robinette, Paul / Li, Wenchen / Allen, Robert / Howard, Ayanna / Wagner, Alen (2016): "Overtrust of Robots in Emergency Evacuation Scenarios": https://www.cc.gatech.edu/~alanwags/pubs/Robinette-HRI-2016.pdf
- Rötzer, Florian (2015): "Goldfische haben bereits eine längere Aufmerksamkeitsspanne als Menschen": https://www.heise.de/tp/features/Goldfische-haben-bereits-eine-laengere-Aufmerksamkeitsspanne-als-Menschen-3232224.html
- Solon, Olivia (2017): "Oh the humanity! Poker computer trounces humans in big step for AI": https://www.theguardian.com/technology/2017/jan/30/libratus-poker-artificial-intelligence-professional-human-players-competition
- Stanford University (2016): "Artificial Intelligence and Life in 2030": https://ai100.stanford.edu/sites/default/files/ai_100_report_0831fnl.pdf
- Statista (2015): "Average of daily internet usage worldwide in 2014, by age group and device (in hours)": https://www.statista.com/statistics/416850/average-duration-of-internet-use-age-device/
- Stern, Joanna / Barna-Stern (2016): "The Dumb, Delightful World of Pet Tech": http://www.wsj.stfi.re/articles/the-dumb-delightful-world-of-pet-tech-1481655316?sf=jkleaad#ab
- Taylor & Francis (2016): "Cognitive Offloading: How Internet is Increasingly Taking Over Human Memory": http://neurosciencenews.com/memory-internet-cognition-4854/
- The Economist: "Democracy Index 2016": http://www.eiu.com/Handlers/WhitepaperHandler.ashx?fi=Democracy-Index-2016.pdf&mode=wp&campaignid=DemocracyIndex2016

- Transparency International: Transparency International Corruption Perception Index 2015": https://www.transparency.org/cpi2015/
- Unanimous A.I. (fetched 05.10.2017): www.unanimous.ai/#
- Varoufakis, Yanis (2017): "Taxing robots won't work, says Yanis Vaoufakis": https://www.weforum.org/agenda/2017/03/taxing-robots-wont-work-says-yanis-varoufakis
- Villeneuve, Denis (2017): "Blade Runner 2049"

0000 0000 ABOUT THE AUTHOR

Patrick Henz started his career in Corporate Information and Compliance at the end of 2007, when he was responsible for the implementation of an Anti-Corruption program in Mexico and several Central American and Caribbean countries. Together with these tasks, he gained valuable insights into global Compliance programs, with a focus on Latin America. Since 2009 in his role as Compliance Officer he is responsible for an effective Compliance program; based on identification, protection, detection, response & recovery and combined with integrity, respect, passion & sustainability. With these means, he defines Compliance as pro-active function, being perceived as guardian, expert and facilitator. The focus is on information to ensure adequate behavior, not only of the human employee, but Artificial Intelligence included.

This includes the regular planning and execution of Compliance Risk Assessments and further global reviews. According an effective sustainability strategy, where Compliance plays a key role, he actively promotes this idea at university workshops and conferences (including the ACI Compliance Boot-Camp 2013, '15 and '17 in Houston). In so doing he became two times President of Honor of Marcus Evans' Latin-American Corporate Compliance Conference 2011 and '12 in Mexico City, panelist at The Economist's Mexico Summit 2015 and co-founder of the Ethics & Compliance Forum Mexico, including editor and co-author of the Ethics & Compliance Manual, published in April 2014.

Since 2013 he lives and works in Atlanta, USA.

www.ingramcontent.com/pod-product-compliance
Lightning Source LLC
Chambersburg PA
CBHW020914180526
45163CB00007B/2722